Sounds
of the
Silk
Road

Musical
Instruments
of Asia

Mitchell Clark

MFA PUBLICATIONS
a division of the Museum of Fine Arts, Boston

MFA Publications
a division of the Museum of Fine Arts, Boston
465 Huntington Avenue
Boston, Massachusetts 02115
www.mfa-publications.org

This book was published in conjunction with
the exhibition "Sounds of the Silk Road: Musical
Instruments of Asia," organized by the Museum
of Fine Arts, Boston, from
July 9, 2005, to January 5, 2006.

For a complete listing of MFA Publications,
please contact the publisher at the address
above, or call 617 369 3438.

Front cover: Detail from Suzuki Harunobu,
The Koto Player (p. 48)
Back cover: *Khọng mọn lek* upright gong circle,
Thailand (p. 83)
Opposite: *Pipa* lute, China (p. 33)

All photographs are by the Photo Studios,
Museum of Fine Arts, Boston, unless otherwise
noted.

Designed by Wilcox Design
Edited by Sarah E. McGaughey
Printed and bound at Graphicom, Verona, Italy

Trade distribution:
D.A.P./Distributed Art Publishers
155 Sixth Avenue, 2nd floor
New York, New York 10013
Tel. 212 627 1999 Fax 212 627 9484

FIRST EDITION
Printed in Italy
This book was printed on acid-free paper.

Contents

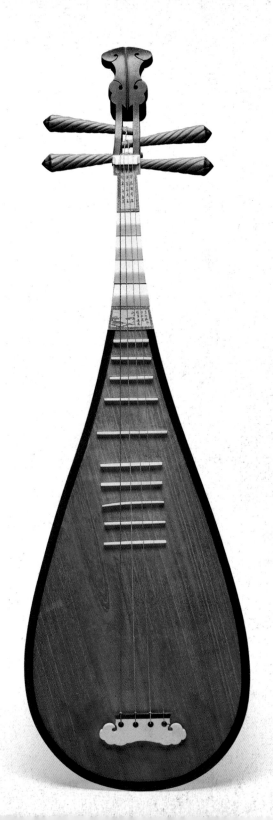

Director's Foreword

The Museum's collection of art and artifacts from Asia is one of its richest and most celebrated treasures. But one element that has hitherto been little explored is a diverse and remarkable group of musical instruments. From a broad array of Chinese instruments that came to the Museum in 1917 to a complete Javanese *gamelan* orchestra acquired in 1990, these objects allow the MFA to interpret the story of Asian music through the artifacts used to create it. Just this past year the Museum was honored with a gift of over thirty superb instruments from Thailand and Burma, donated by the Doris Duke Charitable Foundation. This acquisition was offered at an especially opportune time, and we are excited to debut some of these pieces in this book and in the exhibition it accompanies.

Many of the world's most ancient forms of musical instruments originated on the Asian continent. Gradually transplanted to other parts of the world, they often evolved into differing forms that were tailored to the musical traditions of their adoptive cultures. Likewise, across Asia itself fascinating variations developed among instruments such as zithers, fiddles, flutes, and drums, as each country and region brought to bear its own decorative motifs, mythological histories, and playing styles. The differences make for a particularly rich story, illustrating how a single object can be dramatically reinterpreted in the course of its geographic and historical migrations.

Musical instruments are among the world's most telling cultural artifacts, reflecting an elaborate marriage of technology, artistry, symbolism, and religious beliefs. And as this book demonstrates, the universal language of music has many dialects. I hope that the wonderful instruments described and pictured in these pages will speak to readers and inspire them to explore further the musical traditions of Asia.

MALCOLM ROGERS
Ann and Graham Gund Director
Museum of Fine Arts, Boston

Acknowledgments

The exhibition this book accompanies was organized jointly by the MFA's departments of Musical Instruments and Art of Asia, Oceania, and Africa. In the latter department, I would especially like to thank Joan Cummins, Joe Earle, Anne Nishimura Morse, Hao Sheng, Ann Simonds, and Yiguo Zhang. Not long before work began on the project, the MFA was fortunate to receive a generous gift of Thai and Burmese musical instruments from the Doris Duke Charitable Foundation. I am grateful to Nancy Tingley and Olga Garay for their roles in facilitating that gift. I also want to acknowledge major financial support for my staff position in the early stages of this project, provided by Bradford M. and Dorothea R. Endicott.

The selection of instruments has benefited from loans from local organizations, and I offer my thanks to colleagues at those institutions. The Peabody Essex Museum in Salem generously provided several instruments; I greatly appreciate the valuable efforts of Susan Bean, Nancy Berliner, Alyssa L. Langlais Dodge, Bruce MacLaren, Gerald R. Marsella, Jr., and Andrew Maske. Additional objects were lent by the Boston Symphony Orchestra, with the help of Bridget Carr. Anne Rose Kitagawa and Melissa Moy at the Arthur M. Sackler Museum, Harvard University Art Museums, assisted in providing iconography for the book, as did Thomas Rassieur at the MFA.

Many other people at the MFA contributed to the production of this book. I want to offer my heartfelt thanks to my editor, Sarah McGaughey, who provided invaluable and patient assistance in shaping all aspects of the book's content. I am also grateful to publisher Mark Polizzotti for guiding the book overall, Terry McAweeney for managing the production, and Jean Wilcox for creating the wonderful design. Further thanks go to mapmaker Kristin Caulfield and intern Jenell Forschler. In addition, I extend my appreciation to the MFA's conservation laboratories for preparing a number of the objects for photography and for the exhibition: Gordon Hanlon and Angela Meincke in Furniture Conservation; Claudia Iannuccilli, Anne Peranteau, and Joel Thompson in Textiles Conservation; and Jacki Elgar, Jing Gao, Philip Meredith, Tanya Uyeda, and Joan Wright in Asian Conservation. For the photographs themselves, credit goes to the MFA's Photo Studios, particularly Damon Beale, Christopher Heins, Greg Heins, Thomas Lang, David Mathews, Saravuth Neou, and John Woolf. I also especially thank Alexandra Huff for her indispensable assistance in the musical instrument department office.

I would like to express my gratitude to the following individuals, as well, who contributed in various ways to the development of the book and exhibition: Bill D'Arezzo, Terese Tse Bartholomew, Al Basile, Michael J. Day, Valerie C. Doran, Rick Heizman, Bart Hopkin, Libby Ingalls, Kumja Paik Kim, Drew and Mary Drach McInnes, J. Kenneth Moore, Midori Oka, and D. Samuel Quigley.

Finally, I must express my deeply felt appreciation to Darcy Kuronen, Curator of Musical Instruments, for his guidance and advice on this entire project.

MITCHELL CLARK
Research Fellow, Department of Musical Instruments
Museum of Fine Arts, Boston

Sounds of the Silk Road: An Introduction

The earliest known musical instruments in the world come from the ancient civilizations of Asia. Highly developed lyres and harps dating back some five thousand years have been unearthed in Mesopotamia (present-day Iraq and western Iran). Representations of similar instruments from the same time period have been found in Mesopotamia and Egypt. The evidence suggests that vigorous and advanced musical cultures existed at a very early time, and that a variety of string, wind, and percussion instruments were known throughout the ancient world.

From the beginning, music has been an essential part of life throughout Asia and has played a number of cultural roles. Entertainment was one such early role: we see lyres in mid-third-millennium-B.C. banquet scenes from the Mesopotamian city of Ur, and we find entire orchestras in Chinese murals from the first millennium A.D. Powerful monarchs had ensembles of singers and musicians for their personal diversion (fig. 1). Music was quite simply regarded as a source of great pleasure. In addition, music was an essential ingredient in rituals of all kinds. In classical China, for instance, it was seen as playing a part in the balancing of the empire and of the universe, and was combined with dance and song in ceremonies that honored heaven and earth as well as important ancestors.

Although music was widely enjoyed, admired, and philosophized about, in many early cultures musicians were of a slave class. In some cases, musicians are still considered to be of low social standing. Nevertheless, today performers continue to play musical instruments in all sorts of contexts throughout Asia—to provide entertainment, accompany court rituals, perform religious rites, enhance

Fig. 1. A Persian prince is entertained by two musicians playing a long-neck lute and a tambourine.

Fig. 2. Two players of *gender* metallophones accompany a Balinese puppet play.

the experience of dance and theater (fig. 2), and enliven folk festivals and celebrations such as weddings.

Few generalizations can be applied to Asian music in an investigation that attempts to cover the entire continent. Some traditions—such as North Indian music, for instance—rely primarily on improvisation in extended performances that can last many hours. Others emphasize fixed compositions, the performance of which is most admired when the piece remains identifiable, though enhanced by the performer's personally nuanced playing; the classical tradition of Uzbekistan is an example. In Iranian music, performers are most highly regarded for creating their own suites from existing compositions, bringing the requisite dramatic flair to the transitions from one piece to the next. An Afghan melody may move in wide pitch intervals, exploiting the varied tone colors of an instrument. A Chinese melody may be sinuous, seemingly wandering about, allowing attention to be drawn to the highly varied timbres of an instrumental grouping. One general observation that can be made is that the Western listener, when first approaching the music of Asia, will encounter a variety of musical experiences that require—and reward—open and careful listening.

The training of musicians in Asia is in certain ways similar to the European tradition. In some cultures, young individuals who show an aptitude for music may be encouraged to study it. Elsewhere, where particular professional traditions are regarded as hereditary, offspring will indeed be expected to follow in the family path, and nonfamily members may find it difficult or even impossible to gain access to the family musical secrets. Amateur traditions, when the adept is approaching a musical activity out of his or her own choice and will not expect to make a living from it, are usually nonhereditary. As in the West, instruction is often one-on-one, teacher and student, although groupings of students may learn together from a teacher in a small classroom situation. Training traditionally begins at an early age, since there is a vast amount to learn, process, and experience in becoming a musician. In most Asian cultures, music is learned by rote—taught directly by a teacher who passes on his or her musical knowledge sonically.

Musicians may live their entire lives performing and teaching, and retain everything that they do within their heads. In many cultures, musical notation traditionally plays no role whatsoever. This is, of course, especially true when the very music itself is improvised. In traditions that emphasize improvisation, performances are spontaneously created, based on the deep musical knowledge and experience the musician has developed over the entire course of his or her lifetime.

Various systems of musical notation have been developed, however—some in recent times in response to the influences of Western music, others long before such influences were present. In fact, the earliest known example of musical notation in the world is from Asia. On a mid-second-millennium-B.C. clay tablet, found in the ancient city of Ugarit (in Syria) and inscribed with cuneiform script, is the text of a song accompanied by musical notation. The notation describes the musical intervals to be used, rather than actual

musical pitches. Other notational systems have been developed across the breadth of Asia over the centuries. Many have a mnemonic function, serving as a reminder of the general shape, or specific details, of music already learned orally from a teacher. A similar purpose was behind the original development of Western staff notation, when specific marks indicating musical details were added to the texts of Christian plainchant (commonly called "Gregorian" chant).

None of the traditional Asian musical notations, however, resemble staff notation. Most, like the cuneiform tablet from Ugarit, incorporate aspects of written language. This is especially true of the earliest known musical notation from China, a sixth-century-A.D. notation for an instrumental composition to be played on the *qin* zither.[1] The piece is called *Youlan* (Secluded Orchid), and instructions on how to play the piece indicate verbally to the player that such-and-such a left-hand finger is to press down a particular string at a particular position and such-and-such a right-hand finger is to pluck that string. All this to produce a single sound! The notation is indeed cumbersome, but it developed into a system that abbreviates details of fingering into symbols and arranges them into a musical notation that has the appearance, at first glance, of a Chinese written text (fig. 3).

Of course one can only use this par-

11

12

Fig. 3. Notation for the *qin* zither, shown here in an early-seventeenth-century example, bears a striking similarity to the Chinese written language.

Fig. 4. A Japanese lady plays the *koto* zither on a veranda.

ticular system for the *qin*, and it is a feature of many Asian notations that an individual system can only be used for a certain instrument. The situation compounds itself when traditional notations come together for ensemble music. For example, to notate a piece of ritual music in China, several different notation systems must be combined. Western staff notation, as well as a notational system that indicates musical intervals numerically, have therefore been welcomed into a number of Asian musical contexts. In many circumstances, however, the accuracy that Western notation may offer regarding musical pitch

and rhythm cannot replace all of the details of nuance found in native notations.

In exploring the variety of instruments that are played by Asian musicians, we find many whose general appearance is familiar. The Japanese *shakuhachi*, an end-blown flute, readily suggests the European recorder, while the Turkish *zūrnā* brings to mind the Western oboe. Drums such as the Chinese *bofu* or Iranian *dombak* and handbells such as the Korean *ogoryŏng* are all familiar in their basic shapes. The pair of Tibetan *dung-chen* are, despite their enormous size, clearly trumpets, and the Burmese *saùng-gauk* is, despite its unique proportions, obviously a harp. We might catch glimpses of a plucked instrument such as the guitar in the Chinese *pipa* or the Indian *sitar*, especially given the great variety of forms the guitar has taken in recent decades, or similarly see a hint of the cello in the Iranian *kamānche*.

Less familiar are instruments of such unusual appearance as the Chinese *geling*, Japanese *shō*, Thai *khộng mộn*, Burmese *mí-gyaùng*, and Afghan *chang*. But even these strange-looking objects offer some familiarity in the sounds they produce: for instance, each tiny *geling* produces a chorus of whistles; the *shō* is reminiscent of the harmonica; and the *chang* gives off the familiar twang of a jew's harp.

Some of the instrument types we encounter are specific to Asia, many to particular areas. One example is the East

Fig. 5. A Javanese musician plays the hanging gongs of the MFA's *gamelan*, Kyai Jati Mulyå, at the performance that christened Kyai Jati Mulyå at the Museum in 1990.

Asian long zither, a string instrument that is as primary to the music of East Asia as it is uncommon in other traditions. Long zithers typically have extended, narrow, arched wooden bodies. Scholars of musical instruments usually call them half-tube zithers, the implication generally being that the predecessors of these wooden instruments were tubes of bamboo cut in half lengthwise. Examples are the Chinese *qin*, the Japanese *koto* (fig. 4), and the Korean *kŏmun'go*.

Another distinctively Asian instrument type is the gong-chime, which utilizes a series of pitched gongs played melodically. The Chinese *yunluo* is one example from East Asia, but the real center of gong-chime activity is Southeast Asia, where many such instruments are combined into large ensembles such as the Javanese *gamelan* (fig. 5). A gong-chime intended for virtuosic solo playing is the Thai *khọ̄ng mọ̄n*, with its unusual horseshoe-like shape calling for an almost acrobatic display on the part of the performer.

A number of unexpected materials are used in the construction of Asian instruments. Unusual animal skins form the resonating membranes of various Asian lutes, such as python skin for the Chinese *sanxian* and cat skin for the Japanese *shamisen* and *kokyū*. Precious materials such as ivory are also used, as in the Thai *sọ̄ duang* fiddle. Various structural components are adorned with lacquer, mother-of-pearl inlay, and precious metals, resulting in objects of great visual beauty. The Tibetan *dung-dkar* shell trumpet, made from the rather plain white chank shell, is covered with a rich display of silver foil and semiprecious gems. Bamboo is used in innumerable contexts, especially throughout East and Southeast Asia. In addition to the ubiquitous flutes made from lengths of bamboo stalk, it is found in China in the frame of the *yaoqin* wind harp; in the Javanese *gamelan* as resonators for metal-keyed percussion instruments such as the *gender barung*; and in

India, where it forms almost every part (including the strings) of the *gintang* zither.

Many closely related instrument types exist across Asia and, in some cases, Europe. The evolutions and migrations of music and musical instruments were facilitated by travel along the Silk Road. Ranging some seven thousand miles from the eastern Mediterranean to China, via Mesopotamia, Persia, and Central Asia (with a spur south to India), the Silk Road was primarily a trade route, crucial in the exchange of goods between East and West during the first millennium A.D. (fig. 6). Principal among these goods from the Western point of view was silk, which was prized in the Roman Empire and was literally worth its weight in gold. Lacquerware and spices were other Chinese goods sought after by Westerners, who also coveted precious stones, spices, and muslin from India. Western products that went eastward included glassware, textiles, and items of gold and silver.

The arterial route of the Silk Road was a treacherous one, consisting of mountainous regions and, in many places, desert climates. Caravans were subject to attack by brigands, and heavy taxes were levied along the way. But the advantages of economic and cultural exchange were great. Pilgrims journeyed alongside traders and merchants, contributing to the spread of religious faiths in both directions. And along with all of these, musical cultures

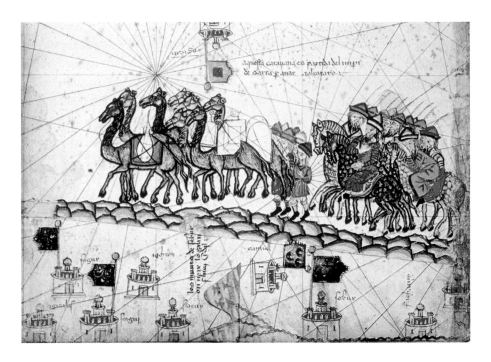

Fig. 6. A caravan crosses the Silk Road in this detail from a fourteenth-century Spanish map.

and instruments were transported across the Asian continent.

In this way, during the first millennium A.D. and later, many musical instrument types traveled from Western Asia to cultural centers in China and India and also westward to cities on the Mediterranean. One notable migration was that of the short-neck lute of Persia called the *barbaṭ*. As the *pipa*, this type of lute was to become one of the principal string instruments of the Chinese (fig. 7). In turn, the Chinese introduced it to Korea, Japan, and Vietnam. Moving to the west, the short-neck lute entered other West

Asian traditions, and with the Arabs it moved yet further west to the Maghreb (Arab northwest Africa) and finally, via Moorish Spain, into Europe.

The migration of musical instruments between Asia and Europe would continue. Free-reed mouth organs, such as the Chinese *sheng*, Japanese *shō*, and Korean *saenghwang*, were once specific to East and Southeast Asia. With the introduction of one such mouth organ in Paris in the eighteenth century, this instrument type— utilizing tiny brass reeds as the sound source—influenced the European development of several important free-reed instruments: the harmonica (packing three or four octaves of reeds into a small boxlike container), accordion, and harmonium.

Certain Asian instruments were an influence upon European types and were then, themselves, reintroduced from Europe to other parts of Asia, completing the circle. The hammered dulcimer, an instrument with a very widespread distribution, is perhaps the most striking example. Originating probably in West Asia during the early part of the second millennium A.D., it spread both east and west, by land and sea routes. By land it migrated well into western and northern Europe and moved east as far as South Asia; by sea it later made its way with European explorers to East Asia, becoming established in southern China about the sixteenth century as the *yangqin* (literally, "foreign zither," fig. 8). From China it was introduced elsewhere in East and Southeast Asia, where it remains very popular. The distribution of the hammered dulcimer therefore has ranged the entirety of the Eurasian landmass and to islands beyond—from Ireland to Japan.[2]

The Museum of Fine Arts, Boston, is fortunate to have one of the more extensive collections of non-Western musical instruments to be found in a Western

museum. Many of these instruments were acquired almost a century ago as part of a large gift from William Lindsey, an MFA trustee. Wishing to make a memorial to his deceased daughter, Leslie Lindsey Mason, Lindsey purchased and donated to the Museum a portion of the instrument collection of the English collector

17

Fig. 7. A West Asian short-neck lute, which would become the *pipa* in China, dangles from the saddle-bag of this Bactrian camel.

and musical scholar Francis W. Galpin (fig. 9). Some 190 of the 560 instruments included in the Lindsey gift, received in 1916, are of Asian origin.

Francis Galpin aimed to be encyclopedic in his instrument collecting, wishing to gather together examples of all instrument types from all cultures—an ambitious undertaking. Galpin amassed an important collection, especially considering the period of his collecting (the later nineteenth and earlier twentieth centuries) and the fact that he himself traveled little, relying on others for non-Western instruments. It is a collection with some particularly strong points, including the Chinese instruments, Northwest Coast American Indian wind instruments, and southern African musical bows. The MFA has been working to narrow those gaps that remain. Countries such as China, Japan, Thailand, Java, India, and Tibet are now well documented in the collection, but others still have limited coverage or—in the case of Korea, Vietnam, and the Central Asian republics—none at all, as yet. In choosing instruments for this book and the exhibition it accompanies, we were able to fill in some gaps with recent acquisitions and generous loans from neighboring institutions and individuals. Covering a geographical range from Japan in the east to Turkey in the west, the selection introduces the remarkable variety of forms and functions of the musical instruments of Asia.

Fig. 8. The hammered dulcimer was imported into China from Europe, in about the sixteenth century, to become the *yangqin* or "foreign zither."

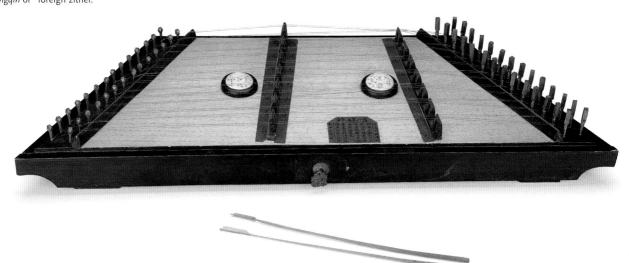

Fig. 9. Francis Galpin (standing at far left) organized this "Japanese Orchestra" for a fete in Hatfield Heath, England, in 1902. Almost all of the pictured instruments, which are Chinese and Sri Lankan as well as Japanese, were donated to the MFA as part of the Leslie Lindsey Mason Collection.

East
Asia

The musical traditions and instruments of the countries of East Asia—China, Japan, and Korea—are intimately related. Japan and Korea are often referred to as being in the Chinese "sphere of influence," since many aspects of their culture and arts originated in China, the oldest civilization of East Asia. This influence is especially true regarding music. Traditional court music and literati music, genres that originated in China and were adapted by Japan and Korea, in particular demonstrate this. Many instrument types, including both those indigenous to China and those that had come to it from countries to the west, are found in Chinese, Japanese, and Korean versions.

East Asian music may be generally characterized as pentatonic—that is, using a musical scale of five principal tones (as differentiated from the tonally richer seven-tone scale predominant in Western music). The music of the three countries is also primarily melodic, as is much Asian music. Harmony, in the Western sense of a chordal accompaniment, is absent in their traditional music, although it has been introduced in recent centuries. What we could speak of as "harmony" in traditional East Asian music has more to do with musical tone color than with supporting chords. Often in a musical performance the instruments involved all play a single melody. Each instrumentalist, however, plays in a fashion that is idiomatic to the specific capabilities of his or her instrument. This means that a flute may embellish the melody with trills; a lute may sustain its sound with tremolo; and an instrument capable of rudimentary chords, such as the mouth organ, may add simple harmonizing notes. The resulting effect is one of great sonic richness, giving the music a depth that may be considered "harmony" in a different sense from that of Western music. The word "heterophony" is sometimes used for this musical effect.

This proclivity for rich tone color is also shown in the variety of unpitched percussion instruments used throughout East Asia, which play a rhythmic role in the musical structure. The emphasis on instrumental tone color does not mean that singing is absent, nor does the stress on heterophony mean that solo instrumental music is less important. Both of these also exist in the music of East Asia, an area that is home to some of the world's oldest continuously practiced musical traditions.

China

Music and the instruments used for its performance play an important part in Chinese culture at all levels of society. Most of the biographies of the early legendary culture heroes and kings show that music was crucial to the development of Chinese civilization. Traditionally, it was considered an essential part of the education of the elite. Music's integral relationship with numerous areas of life is demonstrated by Chinese cosmology, in which aspects of music correspond to the forces of nature in both five-fold and eight-fold systems. In the former, the five notes of the pentatonic scale—which is at the basis of most Chinese music—are seen as corresponding with five seasons (the four seasons plus a variously reckoned fifth season) and five strata of traditional Chinese society, among other associations. In the latter, eight musical tone colors correspond to eight natural phenomena, the eight primary and secondary compass points, eight family relationships, and so on.

China is a vast country geographically, culturally, and historically, and a great many ethnic groups populate the country, each with distinctive musical traditions. Over the course of several millennia, musical instruments have found use in court, literary (fig. 10), and narrative contexts, in operatic and song traditions, and

in the celebrations and rituals of daily life. In general, this chapter will examine the traditions of the Han Chinese, the largest ethnic group.

For much of its history—that is, from the first millennium B.C. through the early twentieth century—China was an empire ruled by an imperial house for which music had an indispensable role. It was believed traditionally that the correct use of music contributed to the stability of the universe and therefore of the empire. To achieve this end, elaborate rituals involving music were developed to honor heaven, earth, and ancestors—giving praise and thanks to imperial ancestors and requesting their guidance for the future. Also important were rituals honoring Confucius (551–478 B.C.), whose philosophical views and systematic organization of earlier religious practices formed the basis of Confucianism, for centuries the state religion of China. All of these rituals became associated with Confucianism and were called *yayue*, or "refined music"; the rituals honoring Confucius continue on a limited scale to this day. The term *yayue* is also applied generally to all music at court and reappears in Japan and Korea as *gagaku* and *aak*, respectively.

In performances of *yayue* a male chorus, accompanied by a large instru-

Fig. 10. A player of the Chinese harp entertains a scholar who has set aside his *qin* in order to listen.

mental ensemble, traditionally sang a series of hymns—each austere in its musical plainness and its similarity to the other hymns. Music was only one part of the lengthy rituals, which also included dance and ceremonial offerings of food and wine. Depending on the ceremony, the dancers might hold feathers, props, or lengths of bamboo painted red, which represented what in earlier times had been actual flutes.

The Chinese ritual music orchestra, seldom heard today, was a large affair with a great variety of instruments of different types and materials. All of the ritual instruments were generally viewed as indigenously Chinese. Correct construction and tuning were required for the instruments, and correct performance on them was absolutely necessary. Percussion instruments used melodically, such as bells and lithophones (instruments made of stone), and those used rhythmically, such as drums and clappers, predominated—at least on the level of sheer bulk of sound. In keeping with cosmological associations, the instruments were arranged physically according to the compass points: bells, for instance, were to the east while lithophones were to the west. In the music itself the bells sounded before the lithophones, figuratively representing both the movement of the sun over the course of the day and a superior intelligence leading other people.

Very few people, and certainly no members of the general population, ever heard this music, despite the important role it was considered to play in the function of the empire. It was confined to the court, as was the music designed for court entertainment. However, music theater had a much greater currency among different levels of society. Indeed, the various forms of Chinese opera are well known today both within and outside China, since the Chinese traveled to many regions of the globe, bringing with them a great love for this music. Of course, in opera the human voice predominates. But a variety of instruments—flutes, fiddles, lutes, drums—also enrich this music. These are the types of instruments generally played by Chinese overseas. Many regional versions find their primary use in opera and other vocal forms, such as sung story-telling and lyric song. The *jinghu* fiddle, for instance, is used only in Beijing opera, where it is prized for the accompaniment of singers.

Another important genre of traditional Chinese music is known as literati music. As its name implies, this is music with literary associations, an art-music genre enjoyed traditionally by an educated class of artists and intellectuals known as the scholar-literati. The principal musical instruments associated with literati music are various kinds of plucked-string instruments such as the *qin* zither and

Fig. 11. Three scholars enjoy *qin* music near a waterfall.

the *pipa* lute, which are typically played solo for small private gatherings and parties. The music played on these instruments frequently has literary themes, sonically describing landscapes or the sounds of birds, for example (fig. 11). Such descriptions are often represented programmatically—that is, the music imitates certain types of sounds. This is especially true of the rushing and halting musical gestures used in those *qin* pieces that imitate the sounds of rivers, a much-loved theme in *qin* music. Although the loftier forms of literati music were typically not the domain of the general populace, its principles of refinement and elegance permeate all Chinese music.

Religious rites and traditions provide a further context for music. Buddhism, Daoism, and Confucianism are the prin-

cipal religions of China.[3] The music of the state rituals, as described above, comprises the musical tradition associated with Confucianism. Both Daoism, an indigenous tradition, and Buddhism, introduced from India early in the first millennium, employ a combination of vocal and instrumental music in their religious rites. The two religions have influenced each other's practices, and they share some ceremonies, hymns, and incantations. The instrumental music for both faiths involves related ensembles of wind and percussion instruments. In the orthodox view, the only permissible instruments are percussion—including a large drum, cymbals, a woodblock in the stylized shape of a fish, and some additional small idiophones—which accompany the chanted liturgy.

Musical instruments were present at

Fig. 12. Carvings from a sixth-century Chinese belt depict a player of the *pipa* lute (who uses the broad plectrum now obsolete in China but still used for the Japanese *biwa*) and a player of the *sheng* mouth organ.

the beginning of Chinese culture. The first legendary hero of China, Fu Xi, who is said to have lived in the early third millennium B.C., is credited with the invention of writing, hunting, and fishing, and the creation of a number of musical instruments. Among the instruments associated with Fu Xi and his consort Nü Wa are the *qin* and *se* zithers, the *sheng* mouth organ (fig. 12), and a variety of types of flutes. Extensive bodies of literature have grown up around some of these instruments, and although legendary, the stories reflect a great deal about the traditional Chinese worldview.

Archaeologically, flutes made of bone dating back to Neolithic times have been unearthed, and instruments made of materials more subject to decay (wood, vegetable materials, skin) have been found that date from about the first millennium B.C. As early as the second millennium B.C., the Chinese were recording textual information about music: inscriptions on the so-called oracle bones—ox scapula and tortoise plastron used for divination—include indications of terms for music and musical instruments.

It was with Confucius and the writings associated with him and his school that highly developed notions of music and its role in society began to emerge. Confucius viewed music as a means of calming the passions rather than as entertainment. The *Yue lun* (A Discussion of Music), a text by a Confucianist philosopher of the fourth century B.C. named Xunzi, contains an axiom that sums up the traditional Chinese view: "Music is joy." What the translation does not reveal is that both "music" and "joy" are written with the same Chinese ideograph (pronounced *yue* in the first instance, *le* in the second). This connection between music and the heightened mental state it engenders is central to Chinese aesthetics and poetics. Confucian scholars also began to apply this associative thinking to musical instruments, describing the sounds of instruments both onomatopoeically and in terms of their effect on a listener. The silk strings of the *qin* and *se* zithers, for example, were described as making the sound *ai* (referring to the plaintive sounds associated with these instruments), which was said to give rise to humility.

An important system for the classification of musical instruments also arose about this time, a system that has elaborate cosmological associations and is still in use (especially in Korea). The name of the system, *bayin*, literally means "eight voices," and by extension "eight musical sounds." The *bayin* classifies instruments by their sounding materials of metal, stone, silk, bamboo, wood, skin (that is, leather), gourd, and clay. As we see from this, Chinese music has its basis in the elemental materials of nature. When instruments of all eight kinds play together

27

觀泉象

Qin zither
China
Probably 17th century
Wutong wood, zi wood
L. 121 cm (47 5/8 in.), w. 19 cm (7 1/2 in.), h. 11 cm
(4 15/16 in.)
Gift of Jane E. Affelder in memory of Paul B.
Affelder   1981.782

in ensemble, as they traditionally do in *yayue*, the totality of the sounds of nature is symbolized.

Representative instruments of the *bayin* categories are bells (metal), lithophones (stone), traditional string instruments (silk), flutes (bamboo), various ritual-music idiophones (wood), drums (skin), the *sheng* mouth organ (gourd), and the *xun* vessel flute (clay). In theory, the individual instruments of the ritual orchestra have a certain equality, each playing an essential and balancing role. In actuality, some *bayin* categories were at an early time recognized as more important than others. This is especially true of

silk. "Of the eight musical materials, silk is the finest," wrote the philosopher Huan Tan in the first century A.D. He went on to say that "of instruments with silk strings, the *qin* is finest of all."

Qin

It is hard to overstate the importance of the *qin* zither in traditional Chinese music. Said to have been invented by the legendary Fu Xi, the *qin* has a documentable history dating back to the second millennium B.C. During the time of Confucius, it came to be associated with statesmen and philosophers, especially Confucius himself. Later it became the instrument

Fig. 13. A musician seated at a table specifically designed for *qin* playing is approached by dancing cranes, which are commonly associated with the *qin*.

of choice of the scholar-literati, obtaining a place in the "four arts" they practiced: music (specifically *qin*), chess, calligraphy, and painting, which has led to the instrument's repeated representation in Chinese painting (fig. 13). Although the *qin* was included in the ritual-music orchestra, it is usually played solo—traditionally in the context of small gatherings of cognoscenti and today often in concert performance. Its repertoire of compositions is claimed to be the largest in Chinese music. However, despite its lofty status, the instrument has never been well known among the general populace, is little known outside of China, and at times has had only a small handful of actual players (although it is currently enjoying renewed popularity).

The standard version of the *qin*, in use since perhaps the third century A.D. and seen here, is made of lacquered wood and is about four feet in length. It is strung with seven strings made of silk that, in addition to being played open, are pressed by the left hand against the surface of the instrument to define pitches. The use of harmonics—bell-like sounds produced by lightly touching a string at certain points along its length—is a highly developed part of the playing technique.

The *qin*'s standard tuning is the five-tone pentatonic scale, as is the music typically played on the instrument. This music generally comprises literary themes evoking poetry and nature. Traditionally, playing the *qin* necessitated an in-depth knowledge of Chinese literature, philosophy, and fine arts (each of which informs the larger artistic context of *qin* music), and mastery of the instrument was an involved undertaking.

Antique *qin* have long been prized as objects of art, both for their cultural associations and for the beauty of their design and construction. Fine *qin* are admired for the elegance and restraint of their general shape and for the quality of the lacquer work. It is the outline that is perhaps the most celebrated aspect of the instrument's design. The classic form, seen here, is known as the Confucian model. As with the ideals of Confucianism, simplicity is the hallmark of this shape, with only slight indentations along each side of the instrument.

Generally, a *qin* has only a bare minimum of decoration. Calligraphic inscriptions (usually poetic) and engraved seals are confined to the underside. The instrument's given name, if it has one, may also be found on the underside. This name may take the form of a historical allusion or refer to the sound—actual or idealized—of the instrument itself. An example of the latter is *Lengqing*, meaning "Icicle sonorous stone," a Song-dynasty *qin* considered to possess a clear, "icy" (*leng*) sound like that of a *qing* lithophone.[4]

Zheng

The *zheng* zither is a popular rather than a ritual instrument. In basic shape the *zheng* resembles the *qin*, and like the latter, it is usually played on a table. Its playing technique, however, is much less complicated than that of the *qin*. Each of its strings is supported by an individual bridge and is plucked by the player's right hand. This means that each string basically produces one pitch, rather than the several produced by the *qin*'s left-hand fretting technique; therefore the tasks assigned to the left hand include only vibrato and bending of musical pitches.

Its relative simplicity led to immense growth in the *zheng*'s popularity, beginning in the early first millennium A.D. The *zheng* is much more commonly played than the *qin* and its music is generally more accessible, which also contributes to its popularity. Although occasionally pieces from the *qin* repertoire may be adapted to the *zheng*, its own repertoire consists more of music based on folk themes. The *zheng* is also commonly found in ensemble contexts.

The history of the *zheng*, both legendary and actual, is closely connected to that of the *qin* and the *se*, an early twenty-

Zheng zither
Jixiang Studio
China (probably Guangzhou)
19th century
Wutong and other woods
L. 98.5 cm (38 3/4 in.), w. 20.9 cm (8 1/4 in.),
h. 12.2 cm (4 13/16 in.)
Leslie Lindsey Mason Collection   17.2056

five-string zither used in ritual music. The *qin* and *se* were traditionally associated in a symbolic pairing: the two instruments in harmony were considered emblematic of domestic concord. However, while the *qin* has remained in use, the large *se* became obsolete, making way for the smaller *zheng*.

According to one legend, the *zheng* was created in the late first millennium B.C. A wealthy and aged man who possessed a fine *se* wished to give it to his two daughters. Hoping they would share the use of the instrument, he was annoyed to find them bickering about which of them should receive sole ownership. Fed up with this arguing the man divided the twenty-five-string instrument down the middle, producing two twelve-string zithers (the *se*'s middle string, the thirteenth, was not played). Thus, it is said, the *zheng* was born. Apropos of this story, "*zheng*" is also the pronunciation of the Chinese word for "conflict"—a far cry from the concord that the pairing of the *qin* and *se* had symbolized.

In reality, the beginnings of the *zheng* were more humble, and it may have had only five strings in its earliest form. Over the centuries the number of silk strings did increase to sixteen, and this was the standard until the early twentieth century. Along the way, *zheng* came to be designed for use with strings of wire, as the one shown here, instead of silk. In the twenti-

eth century the range of the *zheng* increased further still, as the instrument grew to have some thirty strings, rivaling the early *se* in size and bulk.

Pipa

The four-string *pipa* lute has important connections with the literati culture that is otherwise primarily occupied by the *qin*. In addition to being played solo, the *pipa*—unlike the *qin*—is used in a variety of musical ensembles, some purely instrumental and some as accompaniment to singing and sung storytelling. The instrument first appeared in China about two thousand years ago, entering the country from the West via trade routes. It belongs to the large family of short-neck lutes that spans Eurasia, having descended from the same West Asian ancestor as the European lute. *Pipa* musicians traditionally plucked the instrument's strings with a large plectrum. Although its Japanese descendant, the *biwa*, is still played in this way, the *pipa* itself is now played with small individual plectra placed on the tips of the right-hand fingers.

There are traditionally two stylistic themes in the *pipa*'s solo repertoire. One, *wen* or "literary," is similar to music for the *qin* in its emphasis on poetic themes and evocation of natural landscapes. The other, *wu* or "martial," is by contrast concerned with the exploits of military leaders

of China's past. Both the *wen* and *wu*
genres are instrumental music played in
a virtuosic style. Pieces in the *wu* style,
arguably the more popular half of the
pipa repertoire, are often rousing, vivid
programmatic depictions of famous bat-
tles. Although a given *pipa* player may
excel in a certain *wen* or *wu* composition,
the repertoires of most players tend to
represent both themes.

Literary associations are found on the
nineteenth-century *pipa* shown here: two
poetic couplets are inscribed on ivory
veneer on the instrument's neck. Although
somewhat difficult to read, the inscriptions
offer us a poetic context for *pipa* music in
the literati style. Dated to the eleventh
month (called the "winter moon") of 1891,
the first couplet describes the landscape
of the region of Dongting Lake and the
Chu River, west of the city of Shanghai.
Using stock poetic phrases, the second
couplet mentions grand features—"tall
mountains and flowing waters"—of the
river landscape, as viewed in the presence
of the "bright moon and cool wind" of

Pipa lute
China
1891
Teak, *wutong* wood, ivory
L. 99.3 cm (39 1/8 in.), w. 30.5 cm (12 in.),
d. 5.5 cm (2 3/16 in.)
Leslie Lindsey Mason Collection 17.2049

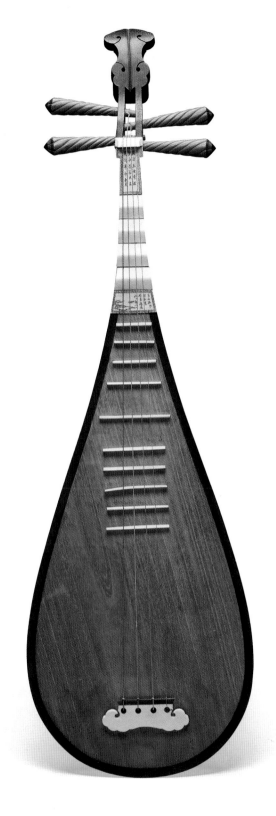

the late part of the year. The text is signed by Wen Shan, a name that means "Literary Mountain"; this could be the pseudonym of a single poet or perhaps the name of a poetry club, with two different members contributing the two couplets.

Sanxian

Long-neck lutes, such as the *sanxian*, are found throughout Asia from Japan to Turkey. Curiously, they are only rarely found in the music of western Europe (the most familiar European form is the Greek bouzouki). The *sanxian* itself has an obscure history and was probably introduced into China about the fourteenth century from Central Asia. The construction of the instrument is quite straightforward, consisting of a boxlike body covered with tightly stretched python skin and a simple fretless neck that pierces the body. The name of the

Sanxian lute
China
19th century
Wood, snakeskin
L. 83.2 cm (32 3/4 in.), w. 14.3 cm (5 5/8 in.),
d. 7.2 cm (2 13/16 in.)
Gift of the National Association of the Colonial Dames of America in the State of New Hampshire
1989.699

instrument is similarly straightforward: *sanxian* simply means "three strings." The strings, which are played with a plectrum, are traditionally made of silk, although nylon is also used nowadays.

With its skin-covered body, the *sanxian* produces a resonant tone resembling that of the Western banjo. It is used in popular traditions, both vocal and instrumental. When accompanying a singer, the *sanxian* player may alter the pitch of the instrument's strings by the use of a capo —a device familiar to guitarists—to help accommodate the voice range of the singer. Visible on this example, the capo, made of bone, is held down at the desired position on the neck by the pressure of the strings that pass through it.

There are different sizes of *sanxian* for different regional uses. In central China a small version is found that may measure between eighty and one hundred centimeters (thirty-two to forty inches); the example illustrated here is of this size. It is used, alone or with the *pipa*, to accompany vocal music and in small chamber music ensembles of the repertoire called *sizhu* —"silk and bamboo" music— where it is combined with other lutes, both plucked and bowed, as well as bamboo wind instruments. On occasion it is played solo, drawing on the repertoire of literati music. A larger version of *sanxian* is found in northern China and is used primarily to accompany singing. The largest of all, a regional variety used by the Yi people in Yunnan province in south-central China, is unique in that its belly is covered with sheepskin and its strings are made of gut. The Yunnan variety is designed to be played by a performer who dances while playing.

Xun

One of China's earliest instrument types, the *xun* is an ocarina-like ceramic flute that is traditionally fashioned in the shape of a goose egg. Ceramic flutes of this type, either with finger holes (allowing for an array of pitches) or without (making the instrument a single-pitched whistle), have been found dating back at least to the second millennium B.C. The *xun* is a "vessel flute," meaning that the body is globular in form rather than tubular (as in flutes made of bamboo). Although of limited melodic range, the *xun* has a deep and mysterious breathy tone.

The instrument's interesting tonal quality has garnered it attention outside the confines of *yayue* ritual music. Although like the *paixiao* panpipes its use is generally limited to *yayue*, the *xun* is occasionally found in intimate performances of Chinese instrumental music. This example is decorated with a flying dragon over a red ground in a manner similar to that of the *paixiao* seen on page 37, and it may have been made at the same time for the same ritual-music purpose.

35

Xun vessel flute
China
19th century
Earthenware
L. 6.5 cm (2 9/16 in.), diam. 5.7 cm (2 1/4 in.)
Leslie Lindsey Mason Collection   17.2114

Paixiao

The *paixiao* has an interesting history as one of the earliest Chinese instruments, having emerged during the second millennium B.C. Its use has generally been limited to *yayue,* and its symbolic associations give it a central importance in that ritual music. The *paixiao* is a form of panpipe in which individual, tuned bamboo tubes are grouped together. It is the instrumental embodiment of an early legend telling of the invention and configuration of twelve pitch pipes and their subsequent association with the voices of two phoenixes. Dating from the third century B.C., the story illustrates the importance of tuning and intonation in Chinese music.

According to the tale, the great Huangdi or Yellow Emperor (who is said to have lived in the twenty-seventh century B.C. but is regarded as a legendary figure) ordered his music master, Ling Lun, to establish a law governing musical tuning. To this end Ling Lun traveled westward to a valley where he found bamboo

***Paixiao* panpipes**
China
19th century
Wood, bamboo
H. 36.4 cm (14 5/16 in.), w. 38.5 cm (15 3/16 in.),
d. 4.5 cm (1 3/4 in.)
Leslie Lindsey Mason Collection   17.2098

of uniform diameter. He cut twelve sections of this bamboo, generating the twelve pitches of the chromatic scale by creating lengths that were alternately shorter (multiplying the previous length by two-thirds, raising the pitch by the interval of a fifth) and longer (multiplying by four-thirds, lowering the pitch by a fourth).

After constructing the twelve pitch pipes, Ling Lun observed a pair of phoenixes, male and female, singing in the valley. He arranged the twelve pipes into two groups of six, one representing the notes of the song of the male phoenix, the other representing the notes of the female, according to the traditional notion of yin and yang. When Ling Lun returned to Huangdi, the emperor ordered him to cast a set of twelve bells based on the pitches of the twelve pipes. Traditionally,

sets of tuned bells used in ritual music are arranged in two rows, grouped according to the yin-yang arrangement. Similarly, the placement of the bamboo pipes in the *paixiao* reflects the grouping into yin and yang.

Although earlier forms of the *paixiao* had as many as twenty-four pipes, the more recent standard form has sixteen pipes contained in a wooden frame. Thus, the twelve original pitch pipes are represented, together with the four highest pitches duplicated an octave lower at the bottom of the instrument's range. From the center of the row, the pipes get progressively longer (and lower in pitch) in each direction outward on the phoenix-like wings, with the "male" yang pipes on one side and the "female" yin pipes on the other. The player holds the instrument by grasping a "wing" in each hand and positioning the row of pipes in front of his or her lips. The frame is often painted red and decorated with mythical animals: this example shows two dragons cavorting among clouds. The Chinese names of the musical pitches are engraved at the top ends of the pipes.

Bofu barrel drum and stand
China (Hangzhou)
1870
Wood, animal skin
Drum: L. 23.2 cm (9 1/8 in.), max. diam. 16 cm
(6 5/16 in.), head diam. 10.5 cm (4 1/8 in.)
Leslie Lindsey Mason Collection   17.2142a–b

Bofu

In China, as elsewhere in the world, percussion is ever present. Percussion instruments—drums, gongs, cymbals, and tuned bell sets—are found in many musical genres, ranging from the ritual orchestra to opera, where they accent the actions of the actors, to folk music, where some ensembles are made up solely of percussion instruments (fig. 14).

One example of a Chinese drum is the *bofu*, a double-headed barrel drum used in *yayue*. Painted bright red and proudly positioned on a wooden stand, the *bofu* is struck on both heads by the

Fig. 14. Itinerant musicians entertain an appreciative listener with their performance on percussion instruments.

player's hands. In *yayue*, two *bofu* provide rhythmic punctuation in the musical performance accompanying a ritual. The *bofu* is similar in shape to other Chinese barrel drums used for more popular musical purposes, such as the *huagu*—the well-known "flower drum"—used to accompany singing.

The inscription on this *bofu*, in gold paint on the instrument's shell, gives the details of the drum's construction: it was one of two made in Hangzhou (near Shanghai) during the autumn of 1870 for the Fuxue Confucian Academy. Since this *bofu* is about half the size of the standard instrument, it may have been made as a presentation object. In the late nineteenth century the Chinese ritual-music tradition was in a decline, and it may be that such small instruments, intricately detailed in all other respects, were only symbolic of the role they had once played.

Yunluo

The translation of the name of this set of ten tuned gongs is "cloud gongs," referring to the cloudlike array of disks seemingly floating in a wooden rack. Ten is the standard number of gongs, arranged in three rows of three with a single gong on top; the scale of notes proceeds from the bottom up. The gongs are high in pitch and are struck with a slender wooden mallet, contributing clear percussive notes to an ensemble's sound.

In the form seen here, with the rack of gongs mounted on a stand, the *yunluo* is used in the *shengguan* ensemble, where it is played together with wind instruments and unpitched percussion in Buddhist or Daoist ceremonials. The name *shengguan* refers to two of the wind instruments included in the ensemble, the *sheng* mouth organ and the *guan* oboe. Although a percussion instrument, the *yunluo* is grouped with the winds because of its melodic nature; among the unpitched percussion instruments are drums and cymbals. The music of such ensembles often has both secular and sacred uses, and the Daoist repertoire sometimes makes use of old popular tunes.

Another use of the *yunluo* is to provide music for outdoor processions, such as weddings and funerals. In that case the rack is mounted on a handle, which is held in one hand by the player. Modern *yunluo* consisting of great racks of forty or more gongs mounted on stands are found in recent orchestral-size combinations of Chinese instruments.

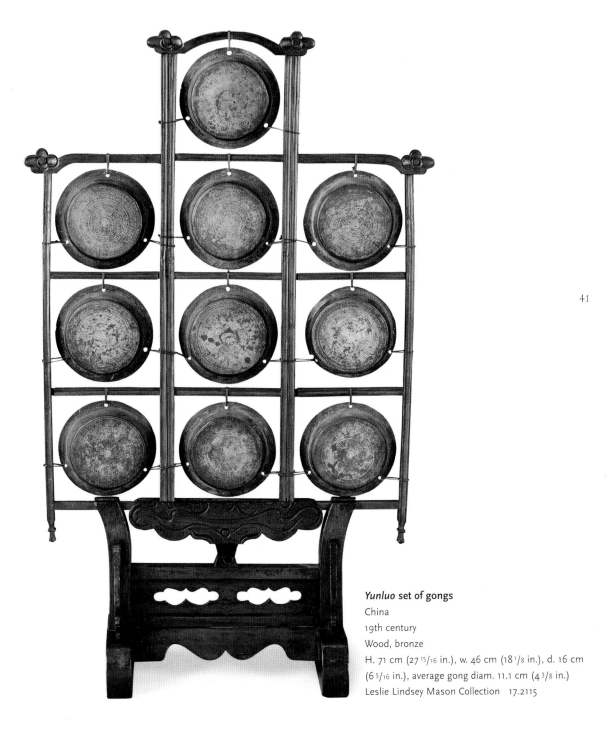

Yunluo **set of gongs**
China
19th century
Wood, bronze
H. 71 cm (27 15/16 in.), w. 46 cm (18 1/8 in.), d. 16 cm
(6 5/16 in.), average gong diam. 11.1 cm (4 3/8 in.)
Leslie Lindsey Mason Collection   17.2115

42

Fig. 15. A street entertainer, with performing hamsters in a box that doubles as a stage, plays the *suona* oboe to attract a crowd.

Soundmakers

Traditionally, Chinese urban centers were rich in a variety of soundmakers, including the signals of street peddlers, hawkers, mendicants, and so on. The construction of residences in enclosed, walled-in areas in older Chinese cities meant that street peddlers and hawkers needed a distinctive audible signal to make their presence known to potential customers. The signals used by peddlers and vendors could be vocal or instrumental; occasionally the two modes were combined. Throughout China, specific instrumental soundmakers tended to be associated with peddlers of certain wares or services, whereas vocal cries varied greatly from locale to locale —presumably because of the differences among the numerous dialects of the spoken Chinese language. The specific non-vocal sounds of the peddlers' signals were therefore immediately, and it would seem universally, identifiable (fig. 15).

One of the best known of the Chinese peddlers' signals is the iron *huantou* clapper, used by itinerant barbers. The example illustrated here is from Beijing. Although it may appear that the forklike sounding body would be struck by the associated mallet, in actuality the mallet is placed between the blades and rapidly and forcibly pulled outwards. This produces a concussive rattle that must have been a stern reminder for those delinquent in getting a haircut.

In addition to peddlers' signals, other utilitarian soundmakers contributed to the soundscape in traditional Chinese

43

Huantou **clapper and mallet**
China
19th century
Iron
L. 33.2 cm (13 1/16 in.), w. 3.5 cm (1 3/8 in.),
d. 3.1 cm (1 1/4 in.)
Leslie Lindsey Mason Collection   17.2127a–b

cities. One of the most curious types is the pigeon whistle, called *geling*. *Geling* were made from small round gourds, or tubes of bamboo or reed, or a combination of the two. Each *geling* was secured to a pigeon's tail feathers by means of a length of wire, which passed through a loop on the underside of the whistle. By various accounts, pigeon owners would use the sounds of *geling* in order to recognize their birds when in flight or to frighten off birds of prey. Whatever the utilitarian intention, the hum of *geling* filling the skies of Chinese cities was a delightful and much-loved sound.

Another sonic pastime long popular in China is flying kites with "humming" bows. A. C. Moule, a scholar of Chinese instruments active in China during the first decade of the twentieth century who may have been the source of some of these MFA soundmakers, noted that there were many "varieties of kite bows and harps at Peking [Beijing] and Nanking [Nanjing], where kite flying is carried on every spring with the utmost enthusiasm."[5] This

Geling pigeon whistles
China
19th century
Gourd
Left: h. 8 cm (3 1/8 in.), diam. 8.1 cm (3 3/16 in.)
Center: h. 4.8 cm (1 7/8 in.), diam. 6.4 cm (2 1/2 in.)
Right: h. 6.3 cm (2 1/2 in.), w. 4.5 cm (1 3/4 in.),
d. 6.4 cm (2 1/2 in.)
Leslie Lindsey Mason Collection   17.2068,
17.2069, and 17.2072

entertainment is still popular in China, the kites being flown in urban parks and country fields.

The Chinese may have been the first to develop string instruments designed specifically to be sounded by the wind. They were attaching humming bows to kites certainly by the tenth century, and the Western wind-activated string instrument known as the Aeolian harp may have been inspired by seventeenth-century reports from Asia of this practice. The Chinese humming bow is usually attached to the back (that is, the upper side away from the ground) of a bamboo-framed paper kite.

A rather complex example of this type of soundmaker is the *yaoqin*. This wind harp is a set of seven straight bamboo rods, each with its own tunable cloth ribbon.

The rods are mounted on a bamboo frame in the shape of a gourd, which is attached to the kite's string. Although the ribbons may ostensibly be tuned, accuracy would not have been very high and the resulting sound was probably an enjoyably noisy racket, rather than a consonant chord.

45

Yaoqin wind harp
China (Shanghai)
19th century
Bamboo
H. 50.5 cm (19 7/8 in.), w. 37.5 cm (14 3/4 in.),
d. 5 cm (1 15/16 in.)
Leslie Lindsey Mason Collection   17.2065

Japan

Because of the conservative nature of traditional Japanese culture, musical styles and genres from very early times still exist in Japan, in some cases in extraordinary states of preservation. Similarly, several musical instruments still retain the form they had when they were imported from China well over a millennium ago, while the Chinese forms have long since been subject to significant formal changes in their homeland. As an island nation that has sought to retain its homogeneity, Japan has experienced periods of self-isolation that have contributed to this conservatism. Consequently, many valuable ancient musical traditions of the Asian mainland still enrich the world of Japanese music.

During the early first millennium A.D., Japan was ruled by a system of clans, later to give way to an imperial state. This was a period of native music, and such indigenous instruments as the *yamatogoto* or *wagon* zither, *yamatobue* flute, and a few percussion instruments were played at that time. A Chinese chronicle of the third century recounts Japanese musical activities, specifically a funeral wake that included singing and dancing. Shintō (literally, the "way of the gods"), a religious system drawing upon indigenous shamanic practices, was organized during this period, and the music and dance associated with

Shintō came to be used as court music.

In the mid-first millennium, music from foreign countries began to be introduced, and musicians from Korea and China brought with them instruments and repertoires; ultimately, foreign court-music genres from the continent became established in Japan. Buddhism and Buddhist chant, or *shōmyō*, were also introduced at this time from Korea. Over the four-hundred-year course of the Heian period (794–1185), the arts flourished and music came to be a prized activity at court.

The music of foreign courts became established in Japan as *gagaku*, with that of Chinese origin called *tōgaku* and that of Korean origin, *komagaku*. *Gagaku* is the "refined music" allied to Chinese *yayue*. As a whole, it is an amalgam of native styles and the styles and instruments imported from the Asian mainland. As court music for ceremonials and banquets, *gagaku* was traditionally reserved for the aristocracy.

The *gagaku* ensemble includes winds (*ryūteki* flute, *hichiriki* oboe, and *shō* mouth organ), plucked strings (*koto* zither, in this case called *gakusō*, and *biwa* lute, in this case called *gakubiwa*), and percussion (*kakko* hourglass-shaped drum, *shōko* gong, and *daiko* barrel drum). Generally, the wind and string instruments are dou-

Fig. 16. Players of the *kokyū* fiddle, *koto* zither, and *shamisen* lute perform chamber music in a *sankyoku* trio.

bled, resulting in an ensemble of about a dozen players, all of whom are seated on the floor. The pitched instruments all play related melodic material, but each in a way idiosyncratic to its playing technique.

Over the course of centuries, the music played by this ensemble has become gradually slower and slower in tempo; commentators on *gagaku* have tended to remark, not unappreciatively, on this otherworldly music's almost glacial slowness. "A block of sound" is how one scholar, William Malm, has described *gagaku*. "It does not move but allows other things to move through it. In this way, it has managed to survive until the present day."[6]

In addition to *gagaku* and *shōmyō*, genres from the early periods that have survived to the present day include the narrative recitations accompanied by the *biwa* lute (described on page 51) and the theatrical form called *nō*. The latter is considered by many to be the greatest accomplishment of Japanese performing arts. In *nō*, theater, dance, and music are synthesized in a creative form that has been highly regarded throughout the world.

In more recent centuries, a greater emphasis has been given to solo-instrument performance. The most important

(and perhaps best known internationally) solo instrument is the thirteen-string *koto* zither (fig. 17), originally an instrument of the *gagaku* ensemble. The *koto* has had a role in Japanese society not unlike that of the piano in Western societies: it is considered an essential part of the refinement of the individual. In addition to solo recitals, the *koto* is played in duet and in small ensembles, often accompanying singers. The instrument is derived from the Chinese *zheng*, imported from China probably during the late seventh century; its large size—almost two meters (six feet) in length—reflects the size of the *zheng* at that time. There are several schools of *koto* playing in Japan, and the repertoire for the instrument has received the attention of some of Japan's finest composers, both in earlier eras and today.

Classical European-style composition, promoted during the period of modernization following the opening of Japan to the West in the later nineteenth century, has also, in the hands of Japanese composers, contributed much to the international artistic community. This is most notable in those contemporary musical works that boldly utilize traditional Japanese instruments in new and creative ways.

49

Fig. 17. A young woman practices the *koto* in an intimate setting.

Wagon (*yamatogoto*) zither
Japan
19th century
Wood, silk
L. 192 cm (75 9/16 in.), w. 23.5 cm (9 1/4 in.),
h. 10.1 cm (4 in.)
Peabody Essex Museum, Gift of Edward Sylvester
Morse E494

Wagon

As elsewhere in East Asia, plucked-string instruments, especially zithers, predominate in Japan. All but one are understood to have been imported from the mainland: the *wagon* alone is considered to be indigenously Japanese. This six-string zither (also called *yamatogoto*; both names literally mean "Japanese stringed instrument") is in fact associated with the origin stories of Japan itself.

According to these tales Amaterasu Ōmikami, the sun goddess, after being insulted by the behavior of her brother, Susanoo no Mikoto, guardian of the underworld, took refuge in a cave from which she refused to emerge. The world was, of course, plunged into total darkness. To coax her out of the cave, the goddess Ame no Uzume danced a bawdy dance outside the cave to music provided by the twangings of musical bows. Amaterasu, her curiosity piqued by the music as well as by the laughter of the other gods of the locale, who were enjoying the entertainment, quit the cave and sunlight returned to the firmament. It is said that six musical bows of the type used to woo Amaterasu, lashed together side by side, formed the first *wagon*.

The *wagon* today retains the form it had by the eighth century. Similar in general shape to the *koto*, the *wagon* is proportionately narrower, as it is strung with only six strings. Tradition calls for bridges made from the natural forks of maple branches, as are found on the *wagon* shown here. Of interest is the arrangement of the pitches of the strings: rather than a series from low to high, the strings are aligned in a specific melodic sequence, which is itself played in set rhythmic patterns. The *wagon* is currently used only in some ceremonial music (now incorporated into *gagaku*) associated with the native Japanese religion of Shintō. Despite this limited use, the instrument is revered for its primal role in the mythology of Japanese music.

Biwa

The *biwa* lute is one of the many Japanese instruments derived from Chinese types, in this case the *pipa*. The form of *biwa* used in *gagaku* (called *gakubiwa*) is that of the seventh-century *pipa*, which was imported into Japan with the other instruments of *gagaku*. In Japan the *biwa* is still played with a broad wooden plectrum, called *bachi* in Japanese (fig. 18), which has since disappeared from *pipa* technique. The *gakubiwa* player sits on the floor with the other *gagaku* musicians, strumming full chords and punctuating them by snapping the plectrum against the leather plectrum guard on the belly of the instrument.

The *gakubiwa* is one of five forms of

biwa in Japan; none of them is common, and all except the *gakubiwa* are used primarily for vocal accompaniment. The *mōsōbiwa*, or "blind priest" *biwa*, is a form that appears to have existed in Japan as long as the *gakubiwa*. It was used by blind mendicant Buddhist priests to accompany the chanting of sutras and epic stories.

A later *biwa* type, illustrated here, evolved in the thirteenth century as a combination of the *gakubiwa* and the *mōsōbiwa* traditions. Called the *heikebiwa*, it was developed specifically to accompany recitations of the *Tale of the Heike*. This epic narrates events that occurred during a period of civil war in the late twelfth century. At least early in the history of the *Tale of the Heike*, the story was performed by specialized *mōsō*. The tale is still occasionally performed, although usually by musicians who are sighted.

The other two forms of *biwa* are regional versions that evolved in recent centuries: the *satsumabiwa* and *chikuzenbiwa*, each of which developed on the southern Japanese island of Kyūshū. Ironically, and happily, a new appreciation of the *biwa* tradition—which had become all but obsolete by the mid-twentieth century—was sparked by new compositions for *biwa* by young Japanese composers after World War II.

Biwa lute
Japan
Early 20th century
Wood
L. 77 cm (30 5/16 in.), w. 30.6 cm (12 1/16 in.),
d. 3.8 cm (1 1/2 in.)
Boston Symphony Orchestra, Casadesus Collection

Fig. 18. Benzaiten, the Japanese goddess of music and good fortune, plays the *biwa* lute using a *bachi* plectrum.

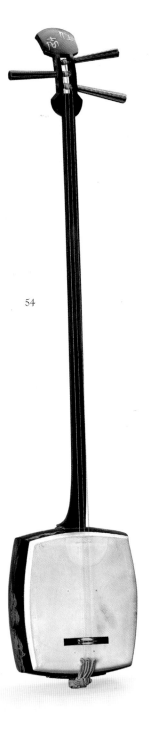

54

Shamisen

One of Japan's most popular and versatile instruments, the *shamisen* is a three-string spike-lute with a cat-skin belly. It is derived from the Chinese *sanxian*; in fact an alternate name for the *shamisen* is *sangen*— the Japanese pronunciation of the Chinese name, meaning "three strings." Whereas *sanxian* is a rather pedestrian name, the *shamisen* naming is quite poetic: it may be rendered as "strings of three flavors."

When it arrived in Japan about the mid-sixteenth century, via the Ryukyu Islands to the south, the *sanxian* began to be played with the broad plectrum used for the *biwa*. It soon became clear that the snakeskin belly of the imported instrument would not stand up to the percussive beatings of the big plectrum. Other kinds of animal skin were found to be more durable and cat skin came to be preferred, with dog skin used for practice purposes. As with most Japanese instruments, the *shamisen* player is usually seated on the floor.

Shamisen lute
Japan
Before 1820
Persimmon wood, *shitan* wood, cat skin
L. 96 cm (37 ¹³/₁₆ in.), w. 19 cm (7 ¹/₂ in.),
d. 8.8 cm (3 ⁷/₁₆ in.)
Frederick Brown Fund and William Lindsey Fund,
by exchange 1992.62

The *shamisen*'s tone is resonant, similar to that of the *sanxian* and resembling the Western banjo. But the *shamisen* has a special feature that further affects its sound. At the top end of the neck, as the three strings pass over the nut, the lowest string is allowed to vibrate against the wood of the neck while the higher two strings pass over a metal fret. This imparts a particular buzzing, called *sawari*, which is a prized feature of the sound.

The *shamisen* finds use in a number of musical genres. It may be played as a solo instrument or in the accompaniment of theatrical genres such as the *bunraku* puppet and the *kabuki* popular theaters. The *shamisen* is also combined with other instruments in ensemble music—most notably in the *sankyoku* ensemble (fig. 16). In *sankyoku* it joins the *koto* and either the *kokyū* or *shakuhachi*. *Sankyoku*, meaning "three melodies," is an intimate chamber music with a repertoire based on pieces originally intended for either solo *shamisen* or solo *koto* but later arranged for the trio ensemble. The *shamisen* is also the quintessential instrument associated with the geisha entertainers, who play the lute with *tsuzumi* and *taiko* drums to accompany singing.

Japan

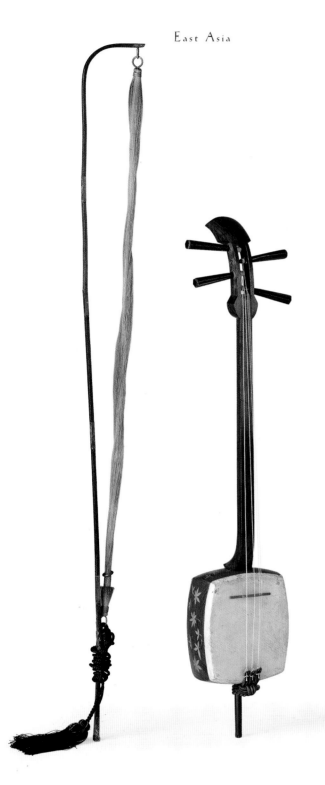

Kokyū

The *kokyū* fiddle is the only bowed string instrument of traditional Japanese music. In shape it is very similar to the *shamisen*, although it is smaller and the spike that passes through the body is longer and forms the base upon which the instrument rests when played. Seated on the floor, the *kokyū* player holds the instrument vertically. The technique of bowing is interesting: rather than passing the bow over the strings, the player holds the bow in one position and rotates the instrument itself.

Although the *kokyū* may have been influenced by a Chinese prototype, there is also hypothesis that the instrument derives from the European three-string rebec fiddle, which might have come to Japan with Europeans in the sixteenth century. Although the *kokyū* was originally used with the *koto* and *shamisen* in the *sankyoku* ensemble, this role was gradually taken over by the *shakuhachi*, and the instrument is seldom played today.

Kokyū **fiddle and bow**
Japan
19th century
Red sandalwood, cat skin
L. 67.7 cm (26 5/8 in.), w. 14.1 cm (5 9/16 in.),
d. 6.7 cm (2 5/8 in.); bow: l. 90.7 cm (35 11/16 in.)
Leslie Lindsey Mason Collection   17.2151a–b

Shō

The *shō* mouth organ is one of the most elegant and unusual instruments of Japanese music. It is a free-reed instrument, with seventeen bamboo pipes nestled in and extending out from a wooden air chamber. Fifteen of the pipes have a thin reed of brass placed at the lower end; the other two pipes are mute (their presence makes the circle of pipes large enough to accommodate the player's hands). The player breathes into the air chamber, and a reed is sounded when the musician covers, with a fingertip, a small hole on the side of the corresponding pipe, thus allowing air to flow past the reed and create a sound.

The *shō*'s Chinese progenitor, the *sheng*, is one of the oldest instruments of Chinese music, and its presence in Japan dates back about twelve hundred years. Although early in its history the *shō* was played in small ensembles, as the *sheng* is in China, its use soon became limited to *gagaku* (fig. 19). The *shō* primarily plays clusters of tones, which contribute a distinctive ethereal beauty to the sound of *gagaku*.

Shō **mouth organ**
Japan
19th century
Wood, bamboo, lacquer
L. 49.5 cm (19 1/2 in.), w. 7.2 cm (2 13/16 in.),
d. 8.6 cm (3 3/8 in.)
Charles Goddard Weld Collection   11.5814

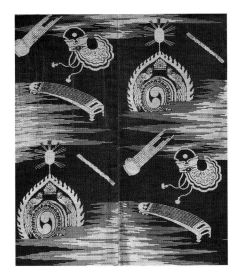

Fig. 19. The *shō* mouth organ is represented on this detail from a *nō* theater costume, along with a *koto* zither, *ryūteki* flute, *dadaiko* drum, and a dancer's headdress—all objects associated with the performance of *gagaku*.

58

Shakuhachi

The name of the *shakuhachi* end-blown flute comes from the length of its standard form, which is one *shaku* (the traditional Japanese foot, slightly longer than the Western foot) and *hachi* (eight) *sun* (the Japanese inch, one-tenth of the foot). The standard modern length is therefore about fifty-five centimeters (twenty-one and a half Western inches), although in earlier times the length of a *shaku* was shorter than it is now.

The *shakuhachi* was developed from a Chinese antecedent, the *xiao*. Several end-blown flutes, considered to be the earliest form of *shakuhachi*, are preserved from the eighth century in the Shōsōin, the Imperial Repository in Nara, Japan. These are made from a variety of materials such as stone, jade, and ivory, and have six holes (five front finger holes and one thumbhole) rather than the five (with one less front finger hole) found on the modern instrument. The Shōsōin *shakuhachi* are of various lengths, the longest being just slightly over forty-four centimeters

(seventeen inches)—the equivalent of one *shaku*, eight *sun* in the eighth century. In fact, it is a characteristic of the instrument that it is called *shakuhachi* despite its actual length.

The *shakuhachi* was traditionally used in religious practices and is strongly identified with Zen Buddhism. In the late seventeenth century the flute became associated with priests of the Fuke sect of Zen. These wandering priests, called *komusō*, were recognized by a hat that looked like a basket and covered their entire heads (fig. 20). Allowed to move freely about the country, the *komusō* played *shakuhachi* in soliciting alms. It is said that, their identities concealed by their hats, the *komusō* additionally functioned as spies for the Japanese government. The *shakuhachi*—made of a hard, stout piece of bamboo—could therefore be utilized, if the need presented itself, as a defensive weapon.

A more secular use of the *shakuhachi* is in the *sankyoku* repertoire, where the instrument is played in trio with the *shamisen* and *koto*, replacing the earlier *kokyū*. Although the tone color of the *shakuhachi* is less nasal than that of the *kokyū*, it still functions as a contrast to the plucked-string tones of the *koto* and

Shakuhachi end-blown flute
Yamaguchi Shiro (1885–1963)
Japan (Tokyo)
Probably 1930s
Bamboo
L. 55 cm (21 5/8 in.), diam. 4.1 cm (1 5/8 in.)
Museum purchase with funds donated by William and Deborah Elfers 2004.130

Fig. 20. The identity of a visitor disguised as a *shakuhachi*-playing *komusō* is revealed by a mirror.

鈴木春信画

shamisen. The use of the *shakuhachi* in *sankyoku* became solidified in the later nineteenth century, during the early Meiji period—one of many "modernizations" that swept Japanese music in response to the influences of the West—perhaps because its sound could be likened to that of the Western flute. The *shakuhachi* is well known in the West and is probably the Japanese musical instrument with the largest number of Western practitioners, several of whom have studied extensively in Japan and are acknowledged as masters of the instrument.

Hora shell trumpet
Japan
19th century
Seashell, silk cord
L. 38.5 cm (15 3/16 in.), w. 21 cm (8 1/4 in.),
d. 14 cm (5 1/2 in.)
Leslie Lindsey Mason Collection   17.2161

Hora

Shell trumpets are found in many parts of the world, their use dating to the Neolithic era. The Japanese *hora* has a history of use extending back at least a millennium. Although the *hora* was used at one time as a military signaling instrument, it is now associated with Buddhism. Descriptions of the *hora* in Buddhist scriptures liken its sound to that of a roaring lion and claim that it will suppress evil. It is still used in some Buddhist rituals, such as the *o-mizu tori* "water-drawing" portion of the Shunie rite—said to be largely unchanged since the eighth century—at the great Todaiji temple in Nara. There, a pair of *hora* is played in the accompanying ensemble, their presence perhaps called for by the ritual's connection with water. The *hora* is most commonly associated with Shugendo, a sect of esoteric Buddhism called "mountaineering asceticism" because it incorporates pre-Buddhist worship of sacred mountains. In Shugendo, the *hora* is used for signaling among adepts in the mountains and for accompanying the chanting of sutras.

Generally, shell trumpets are used to produce a single note. The *hora* is an exception: it can generate three, sometimes even four, pitches. The instrument is made from the triton's trumpet shell (called *horagai* in Japanese), a large shell that is found throughout most of the tropical Pacific and Indian Oceans. In the con-

struction of the *hora*—a process traditionally shrouded with secrecy—the shell is given a brass mouthpiece, placed at the apex of its spire. The silk open-weave covering on this example is a typical feature of the *hora* and forms a carrying bag that may be slung over the player's shoulder.

Gyoban wood gong
Japan
Edo period, 18th or 19th century
Keyaki wood
L. 65.5 cm (25 13/16 in.), w. 16 cm (6 5/16 in.),
h. 23.1 cm (9 1/8 in.)
Peabody Essex Museum, Gift of Dr. Charles
Goddard Weld   E4778

Gyoban

A number of Japanese percussion instruments are specifically associated with Buddhism and are used in monasteries and temples. These instruments are utilized for a variety of purposes ranging from simple signaling functions to the accompaniment of religious rituals. In addition to great booming temple bells are many idiophones, among them the *gyoban* wood gong made of hardwood in the shape of a fish (*gyo*). The *gyoban* is struck with a mallet and is used for calling monks to services. As with the *mokugyo*, a related wooden idiophone in a stylized fish shape that accompanies Buddhist prayer, the fish symbolism may derive from the belief that a fish is awake both day and night and therefore signifies watchfulness. The ball in the fish's mouth is said to represent human desire, which is symbolically exorcised when the *gyoban* is struck.

Korea

It was the Chinese who admiringly commented, in chronicles from the third to fifth centuries A.D., that the Koreans "delighted in singing and dancing." They noted that the inhabitants of the Mahan federation in the southern part of the Korean peninsula commemorated the completion of sowing in the fifth month, and of the farming year in the tenth month, with song and dance. As part of these celebrations of thanksgiving, narratives of the Mahan tribal origins were chanted by a shaman. The Chinese chroniclers also recorded the presence of indigenous Korean long zithers and drums among the other federations in the south. A long zither used by the people of the southern Pyŏnhan federation may have been a forerunner of the *kayagŭm.*[7]

Korean music is strikingly unique: it is vividly rhythmic and is known for the rugged and vigorous earthiness of its tone color. The adherence to the traditional silk strings by players of string instruments contributes to this, as does the vivid reediness of the *taegŭm* flute. Rhythm is an element more vigorously exploited in traditional Korean music than in that of China or Japan. Repeated rhythmic patterns, some of subtle complexity, underlie its musical structures. For this reason, drums are frequently present in perform-ances of traditional Korean music (fig. 21).

As is the case with Japan, Korean music and musical instruments exhibit influences of Chinese music. In addition to earlier introductions of individual instruments, two enormous Chinese musical gifts were presented to Korea in the early twelfth century. Altogether more than six hundred instruments, for use in ritual and court entertainment music, were sent to Korea in 1114 and 1116, becoming the basis for subsequent Korean developments in these Chinese-based musical genres. In the fifteenth century, under the enlightened reign of Korea's King Sejong, a new emphasis was placed on native music, and many indigenous Korean instruments were brought into the mainstream of the orthodox ritual-music tradition, alongside the Chinese instruments.

Koreans view their traditional *kukak,* or "national music," as being in two principal classifications: *chŏngak,* or "orthodox music," and *sogak,* or "popular music." The two categories have a dynamic interrelationship. While they are roughly equivalent to Western notions of classical and folk music, respectively, many traditional musicians in Korea are conversant in both areas; similarly, certain musical genres themselves draw on both.

Chŏngak includes such ritual-music

Fig. 21. A large drum is featured in this ensemble of musicians attending a heavenly banquet.

traditions as the Chinese-derived Confucian music (called *yayue* in China and *aak* in Korea) and the uniquely Korean Royal Ancestral Shrine music. This latter repertoire was developed in the fifteenth century, resulting from the desire to have the worship of King Sejong's ancestors accompanied by music of Korean, rather than Chinese, origin. Art song—settings of poetry in traditional forms by Korean poets—also falls into this category and was traditionally a part of the musical activities of the literati.

Sogak encompasses folk songs, songs associated with Buddhism, and the largely improvised music of the *sinawi* ensemble, which accompanies shamanistic ritual dance. Another genre included in *sogak* is farmers' music, or *nongak*, a percussion-dominated outdoor music traditionally performed in agricultural communities. Farmers' music has given rise to the popular *samulnori* percussion ensemble, in which musicians play and dance in a festive choreography.

The *sogak* category also includes the well-known solo instrumental genre *sanjo*, which draws on *sinawi* yet is allied with the literati tradition. An improvisational form with a suitelike sequence of sections that incorporates existing melodies, *sanjo* was originally developed on the *kayagŭm* zither but may now be played on almost any melodic instrument, with the accompaniment of the *changgo* hourglass-shaped drum. Although *sanjo* derives from folk music, it has become so popular that it is often found in the repertoire of traditional musicians of all types and is now commonly included in concert performances.

In Korea, traditional instruments—whether strings, winds, or percussion—are still categorized by the Chinese *bayin* "eight-sound" system, called *p'arŭm* in Korean. As in China and Japan, long zithers with silk strings are of central musical importance. The two principal Korean long zithers are the *kayagŭm* and the *kŏmun'go*. Aside from those two, there are curiously few string instruments in general use in Korean traditional music. There is no lack of wind instruments, especially those made of bamboo. Most notable are the *taegŭm* side-blown flute and the *p'iri* double-reed pipe, both of which find use in a great number of genres from court music to *sanjo*. Percussion instruments are also plentiful. A wide variety of drums made of skin or leather have traditionally existed, many of them for use in ritual music. Percussion instruments such as drums, gongs, and cymbals also form the backbone of *samulnori* and *nongak*.

Kŏmun'go

The *kŏmun'go* is a long zither said to have been modeled after the Chinese *qin*. According to its origin legend, in the third century a *qin* was sent to the Korean kingdom of Koguryŏ and was remodeled by the minister Wang Sanak into a new instrument suited to the wide vibrato favored in Korean music. One day when Wang Sanak was playing the new instrument, a black crane flew into the room, landed in front of him, and commenced to dance to his music. As the crane is much revered throughout East Asia as a symbol of longevity, this event was considered highly auspicious, and the instrument was given the name *hyŏnhakkŭm*, meaning "black crane zither." Although this was later shortened to *hyŏn'gŭm*, or "black zither," the more vernacular name of *kŏmun'go* (a purely Korean word that may also mean "black zither") is most often used.

Despite its presumed ancestry, the *kŏmun'go* is anything but *qin*-like. In contrast to the bridgeless *qin*, on the *kŏmun'go* half of the strings pass over a series of hefty bridges (allowing for melodic playing) while the remainder pass over individual bridges (limiting those strings to supplying drone pitches). In addition, the music of the *kŏmun'go* is more rhythmic and vigorous than that of the *qin*. However, like the *qin*, the *kŏmun'go* in recent centuries has enjoyed the favor of being associated with literati music and played

Kŏmun'go zither
Korea
19th century
Wood, silk, cotton, leather, bamboo, ivory
L. 153 cm (60 1/4 in.), w. 18.5 cm (7 5/16 in.), h. 14.6 cm (5 3/4 in.)
Peabody Essex Museum, Acquired from the World's Columbian Exposition, Chicago, 1893   E9803

by the intelligentsia. In fact, these artistic circles refer to the *kŏmun'go* simply by the term *kŭm*, the Korean pronunciation of *qin*.

In addition to its use in literati and entertainment music, the *kŏmun'go* — like the *kayagŭm* and a number of other traditional Korean melodic instruments — may be played solo in the *sanjo* tradition, in which the soloist is joined by a player of the distinctive Korean *changgo* drum.

Saenghwang

Like the Japanese *shō*, the Korean *saenghwang* is a free-reed mouth organ derived from the Chinese *sheng*. Its name is a compound of *saeng*, the Korean pronunciation of *sheng*, and the word *hwang*, a term that refers to the vibrating reed itself and acknowledges the big sound produced by the tiniest of reeds. Like the *sheng* and its cousin the Japanese *shō*, the *saenghwang* consists of a number of bamboo pipes placed in a wooden chamber and is capable of chordal playing.

Saenghwang mouth organ
Korea
19th century
Wood, ivory, bamboo, rattan
L. 45 cm (17 11/16 in.), diam. 11.2 cm (4 7/16 in.)
Peabody Essex Museum, Acquired from the World's Columbian Exposition, Chicago, 1893   E9796

As with the *shō* in Japan, the *saeng-hwang* has a very small court-music repertoire: it is only played in duet with the bamboo *tanso* end-blown flute. And as with the *shō*, it contributes an ethereal aura to this music. Although the mouth organ is rare in actual musical use in Korea, it has long been a favorite with painters, who often placed the instrument in the hands of immortals in both folk and literati painting (fig. 22). This popularity stems from an extra-musical association, also found in the other East Asian countries, in which the name of the instrument has the same sound as the word for "birth" (*saeng*), and therefore the instrument is associated with the blessing of numerous offspring.

Fig. 22. The *saenghwang* mouth organ is often depicted in Korean painting because of its association with numerous offspring.

Ogoryŏng

This elegant bronze bell, encrusted with a rich green patina, is of the South Asian type called *ghantā*, used by Buddhist monks in many parts of South, Southeast, and East Asia. The Korean name *ogoryŏng* means "five-pronged bell." This refers to the five prongs (four incurving prongs surrounding a central straight one) of the *dorje* scepter—the "lightning bolt" symbolizing the attainment of enlightenment—that adorns the end of the handle. The bell is said to represent wisdom and in Buddhist ritual is shaken in the practitioner's left hand. This particular example is decorated with representations of the deities Indra and Brahma together with the four Lokapalas, the guardian-kings of the four directions.

Ogoryŏng **bell**
Korea
Unified Silla Dynasty, 8th–9th century
Bronze
H. 20.9 cm (8 1/4 in.), diam. 6.7 cm (2 5/8 in.)
Seth K. Sweetser Fund   34.190

69

Southeast
Asia

ituated as it is between the larger cultures of China and India, Southeast Asia is
an important crossroads in the continent. The region is composed of two major
portions: the mainland peninsula (principally Vietnam, Laos, Kampuchea, Thailand, Burma, and mainland Malaysia) and island Southeast Asia (predominated by
Indonesia, the Philippines, and the island portions of Malaysia) in the southwestern
Pacific Ocean. Influences, musical and otherwise, have flowed into the area from its
powerful neighbors—China to the north and India to the west. The Southeast Asian
countries have also influenced each other's traditions, and these reciprocal exchanges
have been very important musically. As a result, much of the music of Southeast Asia
shares general characteristics despite the cultural diversity of the region. This is especially true in the "gong-chime" ensembles that are particular to these countries. In
order to introduce these characteristic ensembles, this survey of Southeast Asia focuses
on the music and instruments of Thailand, Burma, and Java.

Some mention should be made, though, of Vietnam, a country whose musical
culture is unique within Southeast Asia. Like Japan and Korea, Vietnam made many
cultural borrowings from China, and thus the traditional music of Vietnam shows
more Chinese influence than does other Southeast Asian music. The country was
under Chinese domination for a few periods of its premodern history, and Chinese
music and instruments entered Vietnam during those times. Some of the imported
instruments found continued use there. String instruments are most prominent: one
chamber music ensemble known as *ngū tuyệt*—the "five perfections"—is emblematic
of the Vietnamese love for strings. Although made up entirely of string instruments, it
is a study of contrasting tones and textures. The human voice and its intonations are
also central to Vietnamese music. The extreme degree of sliding and bending sounds
possible on the *đàn bầu* and *đàn tranh* zithers, for instance, are evocative of the human
voice and are highly favored. The Vietnamese have adapted many Western instruments
to achieve similar effects: the guitar, for example, is modified by carving deep troughs
between the frets on the instrument's fingerboard, allowing the player to bend the
pitch of the strings in the Vietnamese manner.

Aside from this notable exception of Vietnam, the Southeast Asian countries are
known, musically, as gong-chime cultures. They are called this because they feature musical ensembles in which sets ("chimes") of pitched metal instruments—specifically gongs
but also other metallophones—are the prominent part of the ensemble. Distinguishing

characteristics of gong-chime music include cyclical musical structures, elaboration and detailed ornamentation of a basic melody, and an emphasis on interlocking patterns played by the instruments in consort. Most familiar to Western listeners are the *gamelan* ensembles of Java and Bali, with their interplay of booming gongs and tinkling metallophones, punctuated by the rhythmic drive of drums (fig. 23). *Gamelan*, together with the various ensembles of Thailand, represent the principal gong-chime ensemble music traditions of Southeast Asia.

Although *gamelan* music has become popular in the West and has received much scholarly attention through the twentieth century, the histories of the music of other parts of Southeast Asia are sometimes patchy and obscure. Because of major upheavals in Thai society during the eighteenth century, little is known about the music of Thailand from before that time. Similarly, information on Burmese music has been hampered by the recent isolationist nature of that country. Nevertheless, interest in these countries' musical traditions continues to grow.

Fig. 23. This selection of instruments from the MFA's *gamelan* shows the variety of gongs and metallophones that are included in a full ensemble.

Thailand

Centrally located in mainland Southeast Asia, Thailand is, like its neighbors, ethnically and musically diverse. The original homeland of the Thai people is understood to have been in southern China. However, as a result of population pressures in China, by the mid-thirteenth century the Thai had migrated into Southeast Asia. Thailand, until recently called Siam, is today a constitutional monarchy and is predominantly Buddhist. Traditionally promoted by the monarchy and its court, Buddhism plays an important part in Thai society and musical culture (fig. 25).

Much of our knowledge of Thai music dates back only to the later eighteenth century, but the few mural paintings and illustrated books that survive from earlier times show that the present-day ensembles, especially the *pī phāt*, have earlier historical precedents. Thailand has borrowed a number of musical instruments from neighboring Southeast Asian cultures. This is most prominent in its absorption of music and instruments of the Mon people of western Thailand and eastern Burma, an ethnic group that has also contributed much to Burmese music.

Thai classical music is played in a variety of contexts, both for court ritual and for entertainment. The *pī phāt*, the most important ensemble of Thai classical music, is called upon to perform the musical introduction to all court ceremonies, such as the important teacher-greeting ritual, or *wai khrū*. Music is prominent throughout these court ceremonies, which can last several days and always include Buddhist rites. Specialized musical ensembles are used for funerals. A few of these ensembles focus on one single extended musical composition that is incorporated into the funeral ritual. Additionally, music accompanies many kinds of theater and, more recently, is heard in purely concert performances.

There is a fascinating and elegant logic to the names, evolution, and organization of Thai musical instruments. The simple, singular forms of instruments are called by straightforward and effective onomatopoeic names. Thus small cymbals made of brass are called *chāp* and *ching*; idiophone clappers made of two pieces of bamboo or wood that are struck together are named *krap*, a word essentially equivalent in sound to the English word "clap"; gongs are called *khǭng*, representing their resonant sound; drums are called by the explosive *klǭng*, oboes by the nasal *pī*, and end-blown duct

Fig. 24. This ensemble of Thai musicians includes players of a two-string fiddle, a large *krajappī* lute (now obsolete), and *ching* cymbals.

Fig. 25. A heavenly musician plays a *krajappī* lute for the Buddha-to-be, who is fainting from hunger as a result of ascetic practice.

flutes by the soft *khlui.* The various Thai fiddles are called *sǭ* (pronounced saw), suggestive of the sound of a string being rubbed by a bow.

The Thai view their complex instruments as having developed out of these simple ones by multiplying and varying the pitches. As elsewhere in Southeast Asia, gongs are combined to create sets that are capable of an array of pitches and are used melodically. The Thai gong sets are generally arranged into circular frames, which are placed flat on the floor so that the individual gongs are all within reach of the floor-seated player. These sets, called

khǭng wong — literally "going circle" — come in two sizes and play an important melodic role in many Thai ensembles. Similarly, individual idiophone clappers are combined into xylophones with keys of bamboo or hardwood; principle is the *ranāt ēk.* In the nineteenth century keyed metallophones were introduced, adding metal keys to the musical ranges of the *ranāt* xylophone types.

In the organization of simple and complex instruments into ensembles, Thai classical music is again systematic. The various instruments are collected into ensemble categories, of which *pī phāt, mahōrī,* and *khrūang sāi* are the main representatives (fig. 24). Ensembles are then generally configured in three sizes of small, medium, and large. It is the presence, principally in the *pī phāt* and *mahōrī* ensembles, of pitched gong sets and keyed metallophones that connects the ensembles of Thailand with the family of gong-chime cultures in Southeast Asia.

Pī nai

In the West we are familiar with oboes as "double-reed" instruments, sounded by means of two slips of cane mounted together on a metal tube, upon which the musician blows. The *pī nai* oboe and related wind instruments of Southeast Asia are actually "quadruple-reed," utilizing altogether four slips of palm leaf as the reed. This gives the instruments a richer, less formal sound than that of the European orchestral oboe.

Made of hardwood, the *pī nai* is a stoutly constructed instrument. Its design is curious in being flared not only at the bell but also at the opposite end, toward the player; additionally, the body bulges in the middle. At the bell end, a wax mixture is added to help tune the instrument. The player uses circular breathing—that is, breathing through the nose while exhaling through the mouth—to produce a continuous sound.

The *pī nai* is the largest of three *pī* oboes, the two smaller forms (*pī nǫk* and *pī klāng*) now largely obsolete. The *pī nai* is therefore often simply called *pī*. Its player is the leader of the *pī phāt* ensemble, and the inclusion of the instrument is the defining feature of that ensemble and the source of its name. The *pī phāt* is used to accompany theatricals—especially masked dramas—and various ceremonies, as well as to provide music for entertainment. Consisting mostly of percussion instruments both pitched (the *ranāt ēk* xylophone and the *khǫng wong* gong circle) and unpitched (various drums and cymbals), the ensemble is characterized by its loud volume. The piercing, nasal sound of the *pī nai* gives the ensemble its distinctive flavor. In the large form of *pī phāt*, two *pī nai* are set against about a dozen percussion instruments, both melodic and rhythmic; occasionally the smaller *pī nǫk* oboe replaces the second *pī nai*.

Pī nai oboe
Thailand
Late 19th or early 20th century
Hardwood, bone, wax, gold leaf
L. 43 cm (16 15/16 in.), diam. 4.6 cm (1 13/16 in.)
Gift of the heirs of Mr. William Lindsey, by exchange   2004.2

78

Khlui phīang ǭ

The Thai consider the *khlui phīang ǭ* end–blown flute to be the earliest instrument created indigenously, rather than adapted from a foreign instrument. As is the case with the *pī nai*, the *khlui phīang ǭ* is the most prominent member of a family of three related wind instruments. It is made from a special variety of bamboo, which is decorated with an attractive floral-like repeated pattern that is burned into the bamboo surface. The flute has seven finger holes on the front (the hole below the seventh finger hole is not played) and one thumbhole on the back. An additional hole on the side is covered by a mirliton, a thin membrane that imparts a special kazoolike reediness to the tone.

The *khlui phīang ǭ* is the featured wind instrument of the *mahōrī* ensemble, in which it is joined by the *sǭ sam sai* three-string fiddle (played by the ensemble leader) and percussion instruments. The *mahōrī* is softer in volume than the *pī phāt* ensemble, uses smaller versions of the xylophone and gong circle, and is used to play chamber music.

Khlui phīang ǭ end-blown flute
Thailand
Mid-20th century
Bamboo
L. 44.1 cm (17 3/8 in.), diam. 2.8 cm (1 1/8 in.)
Helen and Alice Colburn Fund 1984.281

Thōn mahōrī

A variety of drums found in West Asia are called goblet drums, referring to the instruments' gobletlike shape (see, for example, the Iranian *dombak* on page 140). Thailand's *thōn* goblet drum type may have originated there. One type of *thōn*, called *thōn chātrī*, has a body of

Thōn mahōrī goblet drum
Thailand
Bangkok period, late 19th – early 20th century
Wood, mother-of-pearl, string, lacquer, leather
H. 38 cm (15 1/4 in.), diam. 24 cm (9 1/2 in.)
Gift of Doris Duke's Southeast Asian Art Collection
2004.406

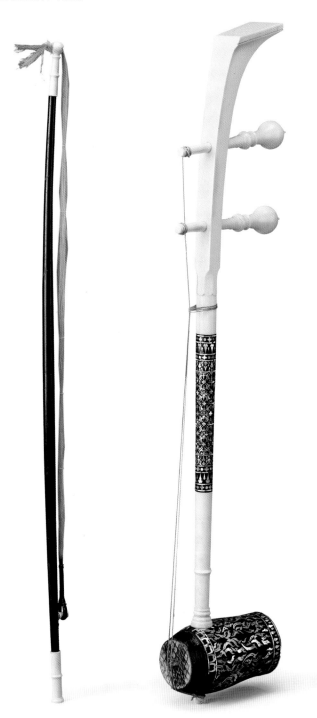

hardwood and is played in pairs in the *pī phāt chātrī* ensemble that accompanies shadow-puppet plays. The other type, the *thōn mahōrī*, is made of ceramic and is used in the *mahōrī* and *khrūang sāi* ensembles. It is played with the drumhead vertical to the floor and is paired with a frame drum called *rammanā mahōrī*, held in a similar fashion. Often the two drums are played by the same musician, and the pair provides rhythmic punctuation to ensemble music.

The intricate decoration on this *thōn mahōrī* is created with inlaid mother-of-pearl, commonly used for decoration in Thailand. When not being played, the drum rests on its head, as illustrated here, and it is in this position that the central image of the seated Buddha is seen right side up. The *rammanā mahōrī* associated with this *thōn* also bears a mother-of-pearl decoration—an image of a Buddhist celestial being called *apsara*—that is correctly seen when that instrument rests drumhead upwards.[8]

Sǫ duang fiddle and bow
Thailand
Bangkok period, late 19th–early 20th century
Ivory, mother-of-pearl, lacquer, string
L. 71 cm (28 in.), w. 6.5 cm (2 1/2 in.),
d. 18.5 cm (7 1/4 in.)
Gift of Doris Duke's Southeast Asian Art Collection
2004.416a–b

Sǫ duang

The *sǫ duang* is one of three elegant forms of fiddles used in Thai classical music. It shares a distinctive feature with some Chinese fiddles: the bow passes between the fiddle's two strings and cannot be separated from the instrument. In this configuration the player, who holds the instrument upright, needs only to exert a slight pressure to one side or the other to select the string to be played.

Much of this *sǫ duang* is made of ivory, and intricate mother-of-pearl inlay decorates the instrument's body and a portion of the neck. The belly, as is typical, is made from python skin. It is said that the instrument is so named because its shape resembles a type of trap called *duang*, used to snare a particular edible lizard prized in northern Thailand.

The *sǫ duang* is joined by the *sǫ ū*, a larger Thai fiddle, in the *khrūang sāi*.[9] This chamber-music ensemble features string instruments in combination with flutes and percussion. *Khrūang sāi* is a more recent institution than the other Thai ensembles, and its large form occasionally includes instruments of foreign origin, such as the Western violin and accordion. The high pitch and penetrating tone of the *sǫ duang* give the instrument the prominent place in *khrūang sāi*.

Khǭng mǭn

The *khǭng mǭn* is one of the instruments associated with the Mon people of western Thailand. This aggregation of gongs has a range of pitches identical to the more common *khǭng wong* gong circle. But rather than resting on the ground, the wooden frame holding the gongs extends upwards into the air like a horseshoe stood on end. The stocky frame of the *khǭng mǭn* is typically carved with the image of a mythological celestial musician—half human, half bird—called *kin nōn*. The creature's head is reverently referred to by the player as the "face of the god." The whole frame is usually decorated lavishly with gold paint and glass inlay.

Khǭng mǭn are featured in a specialized type of *pī phāt* ensemble used for funeral music called the *pī phāt mǭn*. Although the instruments and repertoire of *pī phāt mǭn* are associated with the Mon people and are derived from the music of that ethnic group, in Thai classical music the musicians of *pī phāt mǭn* are Thai. The *pī phāt mǭn* is similar to a medium-size *pī phāt* ensemble but makes some important substitutions. Principal among these are the replacement of the *pī nai* with the larger *pī mǭn* oboe and the two sizes of *khǭng wong* gong circles by two sizes of *khǭng mǭn*. The *khǭng mǭn* shown here is the smaller (*lek*) of the two sizes.

Khŏng mŏn lek **upright gong circle**
Thailand
Bangkok period, late 19th–early 20th century
Wood, gilt, glass inlay, lacquer, ivory, brass, leather
L. 132 cm (52 in.), w. 23 cm (9 in.),
h. 99 cm (39 in.)
Gift of Doris Duke's Southeast Asian Art Collection
2004.402

Fig. 26. This Burmese ensemble features players of
the *saùng-gauk* arched harp, *mí-gyaùng* crocodile-
shaped zither, and *pat-talà* xylophone.

Burma

Because of Burma's political isolation, it has one of the least well-known musical traditions in Southeast Asia. Formerly part of the British Empire, Burma (presently also called Myanmar) gained independence after the Second World War. Internal strife and an increasingly isolationist government have contributed to the country's remoteness. But what glimpses we have of Burmese music show it to be quite extraordinary. Instruments such as the *pat-waìng* tuned drum-chime, *mí-gyaùng* zither, *saùng-gauk* arched harp, and *pat-talà* metallophone, as well as the uniquely Burmese *hsaìng-waìng* ensemble, imbue Burmese music with unusual sounds and a rich variety of visual forms.

There are two essential types of ethnic Burmese music: "indoor," a soft-sounding chamber music, and "outdoor," a loud, even boisterous, style for accompanying theater and rituals. This dual distinction of indoor and outdoor may be found in many music cultures, where certain soft-sounding instruments would be difficult to hear outdoors while louder instruments would overpower a listener in an indoor situation.

Although Burma shares borders with both China and India, only a few aspects of Burmese music seem to be derived from these cultures. The *pat-waìng* and the

saùng-gauk have precedents in India and represent some of the few Indian influences still present among instruments in Southeast Asian music. India was also the direct source of Buddhism, which is today prevalent in Burma.

Western musical influences have been felt in Burma for some two centuries, and certain Western instruments have been adopted. The piano was probably introduced by the British in the early to mid-nineteenth century as a presentation object to the ruling powers and was greatly enjoyed at court. It appears to have replaced the indigenous *sandeya*, a string instrument, possibly a hammered dulcimer, about which little is known. A similar situation occurred when the Western violin took the place of the Burmese *tayaw* fiddle. Such replacements may be the result of a perceived greater versatility in the new instrument and a basic attraction of things foreign and exotic—and in the case of the piano, the appeal of European mechanical ingenuity.

The central musical ensemble of Burma is the *hsaìng-waìng*. Used for outdoor music, this ensemble features many instrument types, including tuned gongs, oboes, cymbals, and various wooden idiophones. Particularly remarkable is the lead instrument, the *pat-waìng*, after which the ensemble is named. This large set of tuned barrel drums enclosed in a circular frame is played melodically. Various sets of tuned gongs are also included in *hsaìng-waìng*, allying the ensemble to the other gong-chime traditions of Southeast Asia.

The *hsaìng-waìng* is extremely popular throughout Burma, playing a prominent role in accompanying theater and performing at all sorts of social events including weddings, the ordination of monks, temple festivals, and the Burmese *nat pwè* "spirit festival." Most *hsaìng-waìng* troupes include a featured performer, usually male, who functions as singer, dancer, and comedian. With its sudden shifts of tempo and seemingly chaotic musical texture, the *hsaìng-waìng* has a quality of sophisticated wit and is one of the most distinctive musical ensembles of Southeast Asia.

Mí-gyaùng

The earliest description of Burmese music comes from China. Documents dating back to the turn of the ninth century note that musicians of the Burmese Pyu kingdom visited the Chinese court as part of a diplomatic mission. Among the indoor-music instruments they brought with them was a "lizard-head zither," which may well be an ancestor of the Burmese *mí-gyaùng*.

In the form of a crocodile (from which the instrument receives its native name), the three-string *mí-gyaùng* is one of the most wonderful examples of zoomorphic imagery in all of Asia. An origin myth for the creation of the instrument relates that its repertoire was derived from the melodious humming of Nga Moe Yeik (meaning "Rain Cloud"), a super-

Mí-gyaùng zither
Burma
Mid-19th century
Tropical hardwood
L. 113.8 cm (44 ¹³/₁₆ in.), w. 15.6 cm (6 ⅛ in.),
h. 15.9 cm (6 ¼ in.)
Arthur Tracy Cabot Fund   1993.11

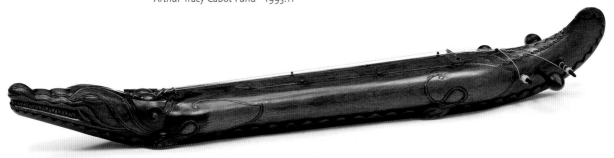

natural being in the form of a crocodile who introduced the *mí-gyaùng* to humans. The example shown here is intricately carved from a single piece of hardwood and painstakingly hollowed out through a narrow slit in the belly. Ornately painted examples also exist, some decorated with glass inlay. On some instruments the crocodile's head and tail are detachable.

The *mí-gyaùng* is played on the ground, traditionally in an ensemble context (see fig. 26). At present only the Mon people, an ethnic group of eastern Burma, play the *mí-gyaùng*, and it is rare even among them.[10] The modern use of the Western guitar—played flat on the floor with a slide—by the ethnic Burmese may be a continuation of the playing techniques of the *mí-gyaùng*, adapted for a modern instrument.[11]

Saùng-gauk

Perhaps the principal solo instrument of Burma is its arched harp, called *saùng-gauk*. Although historically harps were found throughout much of Asia, the *saùng-gauk* is virtually the only Asian harp remaining in general use. It is an instrument of elegant beauty. The graceful turn of its neck is the natural curve of a root of the *shà* tree, with which construction of the instrument begins. A body of padauk wood is added to the neck and covered with a belly made of deerskin. The body is then lacquered and the belly painted. Thirteen strings of twisted silk are individually knotted at the string holder on the body and extended to the neck, where they are held in place by tuning cords of red cotton, each of which ends in a tassel.

In addition to its eminence as a vir-

Saùng-gauk arched harp
Southern Burma
Mid-19th century
Padauk wood, *shà* wood, deerskin
L. 81 cm (31 7/8 in.), w. 16 cm (6 5/16 in.),
h. 66 cm (26 in.)
Samuel Putnam Avery Fund 1992.5a

tuosic solo instrument, the *saùng-gauk* is used to accompany classical song. Both of these repertoires place the instrument in the category of indoor music. Although the *saùng-gauk* was formerly associated with the Burmese court, its use now survives through private patronage, public performances, and recordings. The gentle, though vigorous, sound of the *saùng-gauk* heard on recordings or in films is often a Westerner's introduction to the music of Burma. A similar arched harp may also have been one of the first Burmese instruments with which the ninth-century Chinese courtiers became familiar.

Pat-talà

Another celebrated instrument in Burma is the *pat-talà*, which can be found in both xylophone and metallophone forms. As a solo instrument in its xylophone form, the *pat-talà* is a vehicle for great virtuosity on the part of the performer. It can also be played in small indoor ensembles, often accompanying singers. Additionally, it is sometimes used in the outdoor-music ensemble that accompanies the theatrical genre *anyeìn*; there, it is played by the ensemble leader.

The MFA's *pat-talà* is an exceptional example of the instrument: its ornately carved case is in the form of a dragon and is covered with gold lacquer. This unusual form implies that it was designed for presentation as a gift or perhaps created for a wealthy Chinese patron, as the dragon is a symbol of central importance in Chinese imagery. The typical form of *pat-talà* is much simpler, with a simple pedestal and a curved plain trough supporting bamboo keys (see fig. 26).

Also unusual is that this example's keys are made of iron instead of the more usual bamboo. Although seldom encountered, the metallophone form of *pat-talà* is sometimes used in the *hsaìng-waìng* ensemble, taking the place of the usual *kyì-waìng* gong circle.

Pat-talà **metallophone**
Burma
Late 19th – early 20th century
Wood, lacquer, lead, gilt, glass inlay
L. 178 cm (70 in.), w. 35.5 cm (14 in.), h. 88.5 cm
(34 3/4 in.)
Gift of Doris Duke's Southeast Asian Art Collection
2004.418
Photograph © 2002 Doris Duke Charitable
Foundation

Java

Java is one of the largest of the islands of the Indonesian archipelago and, as home to the majority of the population, one of the most densely populated places on earth. It is also the political center of the Republic of Indonesia: the Javanese city of Jakarta, with more than seventeen million people, is the Indonesian capitol. Originally Hindu in religion, the Javanese—along with much of Indonesia—converted to Islam several centuries ago. However, earlier Hindu and Buddhist beliefs have been combined with Islam in a uniquely Indonesian syncretic form. Though Indonesia is now a republic, many of the court rituals associated with the royal past are still practiced.

Some of the most notable of the gong-chime ensembles of Southeast Asia have developed in the island cultures of Indonesia. These are the *gamelan* orchestras, found principally on the islands of Java (where there are different *gamelan* traditions in different parts of the island), Bali, and Madura, as well as elsewhere in Indonesia, mostly where Javanese have settled. The term *gamelan* refers to ensembles of a variety of instruments, predominantly bronze gongs and metallophones. Although the Indonesian word *gamelan* appears to be related to the Javanese word for bronze, in some cases other sonorous materials such as iron, wood, or bamboo are substituted for bronze.

The *gamelan* ensembles may have their origins in the simple bronze drums that emerged during the first millennium B.C. in mainland Southeast Asia. These large drumlike idiophones were made entirely of bronze and suspended like gongs. In some parts of Southeast Asia such drums were decorated with images of frogs and called "frog drums," the association of the frog with water imparting to the instruments a power for evoking rain. The bronze drums may also have been used originally as signaling instruments and later collected together into a set, or chime, of up to sixteen drums.

Bronze objects were introduced from the Southeast Asian mainland into Indonesia late in the first millennium B.C. Not all of the metals used in the bronze alloy were readily available in Java, and initially all bronze objects were acquired from the mainland as spoils of war. The rarity of bronze meant that objects made from it were greatly valued and considered to have supernatural powers—an aspect that lingers in the veneration still attached to *gamelan* instruments. The gongs of the *gamelan* may have developed from Javanese attempts to imitate the bronze drums. Learning the techniques of working bronze

themselves, gongsmiths in Java perfected their art and acquired a reputation throughout Southeast Asia.

Gamelan is the principal musical tradition in Java, pervasive throughout the culture. The most ancient type of *gamelan* is *gamelan munggang,* a name that appears in a Javanese myth in which the Hindu god Siva commands that a set of gongs be made, thus creating the first music. Playing a simple three-note scale, *gamelan munggang* are still used in court ceremonies and are regarded as profoundly sacred entities. The music of *gamelan* fulfills a broad range of functions, from enticing rain for rice crops, to accompanying dance and puppet theater, to providing the primary activity of *klenengan,* nightlong gatherings of *gamelan* musicians.

Gamelan

In Central Javanese *gamelan,* tuned gongs predominate, ranging from the enormous *gong ageng*—one meter (over three feet) in diameter—down to small pot-shaped gongs played in sets, together with a variety of other metallophones. To these are added a xylophone, flute, string instruments, and a selection of drums. In performance, a solo female singer and a male chorus are

Fig. 27. Javanese musicians play the MFA's *gamelan* at its first performance after acquisition by the Museum in 1990.

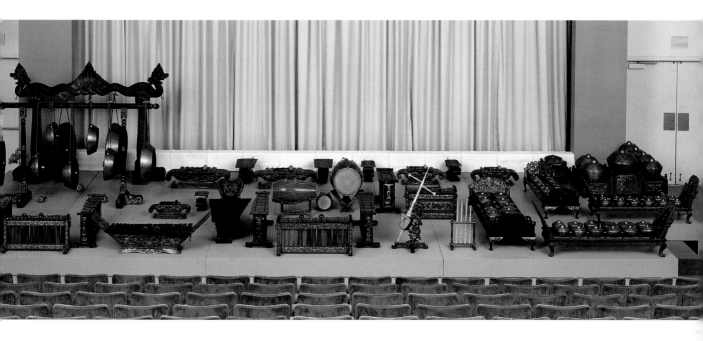

also included. All of the performers are seated on the floor as, at least in traditional contexts, is the audience (fig. 27). Traditionally, the *gamelan* instruments are set up in a square or rectangular building with a peaked roof supported by columns and open on all sides (or on three sides, if it is connected to a larger building).

Complete Javanese *gamelan* comprise two entire sets of instruments, one for each of the Javanese modal systems (although a few instruments can serve both modes), in a full complement called *gamelan lengkap*. These two modal systems, the pentatonic (five-tone) *slendro* and the heptatonic (seven-tone) *pelog*, may be

generally likened, in their role of providing tonal contrast, to the major and minor modes of Western music. The two modes are not played simultaneously, although they may alternate within a given performance. The pairs of *slendro* and *pelog* instruments are set close together in the orchestral layout, usually at a ninety-degree angle, so that players can make a quick switch from one tuning system to the other (fig. 28). Ideally, all of the bronze instruments of a given Javanese *gamelan* are made of the same alloy and are tuned together, creating an individual ensemble that will sound like no other.

Gamelan music is a social activity

Fig. 28. The Museum's *gamelan* set up in playing position on a concert stage.

central to the texture of Javanese life. The ensembles are often owned by communities or families, and the music calls for a group harmony in the tasks of learning and playing the repertoire. In this context, Javanese encounter *gamelan* repeatedly from early childhood. Musical involvement is encouraged for beginners, and as the different instruments of the *gamelan* call for various levels of skill, novice players can perform with more experienced musicians. The serious student of *gamelan* will eventually learn all the instruments and be able to move from one to another with ease.

Increasingly, there are music schools in Java that teach *gamelan* in addition to the allied arts of dance and puppet theater. Though traditionally transmitted orally, *gamelan* music has acquired various notational systems over the past century or so, of which the most commonly used is the *kepatihan* "cipher" notation. In this system, numbers are used to represent the pitches of the scale. Experienced *gamelan* players, even if they have learned their repertoire by means of *kepatihan* notation, still tend to play from memory.

To the musicians who play it and the listeners who hear it, a *gamelan* is a sacred collective entity with its own personality, soul, and history. The individual instruments of the *gamelan* are considered to be sacred objects. Human beings should never step over them, as that would be a sign of disrespect, but rather walk around them. The instruments are regarded as dwelling places for sacred spirits, and the most revered of all is the great *gong ageng*. So venerated are the gongs, that holy water in which old *gong ageng* have been ceremonially washed is sold for healing purposes.[12] A fine *gamelan* is even given a personal name. The name of the Central-Javanese *gamelan* in the collection of the Museum of Fine Arts is Kyai Jati Mulyå, meaning "Venerable Truly Noble."

Kyai Jati Mulyå is from the city of Blora in north Central Java. It is a complete *gamelan*, with both *slendro* and *pelog* sets of instruments represented. The *slendro* set is the earlier of the two, made in 1840 for a wealthy Chinese patron living in Java. Its teak casework is richly decorated with floral bas-relief carving, painted red with gilded details. This decoration includes dragon images with features of both Chinese and Javanese iconography. The *pelog* set is from about 1876. It features a minimum of carving and is painted black. The bronze work of Kyai Jati Mulyå is of excellent quality, and the four *gong ageng* are regarded as extraordinarily fine examples of the type.

The bronze gongs and other metallophones that form the core of Kyai Jati Mulyå and other Javanese *gamelan* center around the hanging *gong ageng*, whose deep, complex bass note anchors the

***Gong ageng* gongs and stand**
Central Java, Indonesia
1840 and before 1867
Teak, bronze
Stand: l. 262 cm (103 1/8 in.), w. 71.5 cm (28 1/8 in.),
h. 189.5 cm (74 5/8 in.)
Gift of Mr. and Mrs. Bradford M. Endicott and Mr.
and Mrs. Richard M. Fraser in honor of Jan and
Suzanne Fontein, and the Frank B. Bemis Fund
1990.556a, 1990.574b, 1990.556c–e

Slenthem metallophone
Central Java, Indonesia
1840
Teak, bronze
L. 73.5 cm (28 ^{15}/$_{16}$ in.), w. 35.5 cm (14 in.),
h. 46 cm (18 ^{1}/$_{8}$ in.)
Gift of Mr. and Mrs. Bradford M. Endicott and Mr.
and Mrs. Richard M. Fraser in honor of Jan and
Suzanne Fontein, and the Frank B. Bemis Fund
1990.540

96

ensemble sonically and temporally. The large size of the *gong ageng*, referred to simply as the "big gong," belies its relatively light construction. In fact, it is one of the aspects of pitched idiophones that less material mass, and therefore greater flexibility, can lead to lower musical pitch.

Additional, smaller hanging gongs contribute middle-range pitches to the ensemble sound. Gongs of a different type, smaller yet, are laid flat on supporting cords rather than being hung. These are called kettle gongs for their distinctive shape and include the *kenong*, of which the *kenong japan* is the largest example. A number of metallophones with arrangements of bronze bars or keys, such as the *slenthem*, supply the basic form of the ensemble melody. Among these metallophones, the most important

Gender barung metallophone
Central Java, Indonesia
1840
Teak, bronze
L. 98.5 cm (38 3/4 in.), w. 34.5 cm (13 9/16 in.),
h. 44.5 cm (17 1/2 in.)
Gift of Mr. and Mrs. Bradford M. Endicott and Mr. and Mrs. Richard M. Fraser in honor of Jan and Suzanne Fontein, and the Frank B. Bemis Fund
1990.538

musical role is given to the *gender*. The *gender* are instruments of extended ranges that are played in a two-voice style (a mallet in each hand), and their performance includes much improvisation.

One of the most important instruments of the *gamelan*, generally played by a principal member of the ensemble, is the *rebab* spike fiddle. The *rebab* of Kyai Jati Mulyå is very precious, being made of ivory. The player sits on the floor, the *rebab* resting on its spike. As with the Japanese *kokyū*, the *rebab* is played with the bow held in one position while the instrument itself is rotated back and forth. The animal-skin belly of the instrument contributes to the *rebab*'s nasal tone color, which is considered ideal for accompanying the female vocalist who performs with the *gamelan*. It is often the *rebab* that gives

a solo introduction to a *gamelan* performance, and sometimes it lingers at the end of a postlude as well.

Two wire-strung zithers and a duct flute may also be included in a Javanese *gamelan*. Last but not least are the drums. Three sizes of *kendhang*, doubled-headed barrel-shaped drums with heads tightened by laces, are played by the *gamelan* ensemble leader. The drummer plays stylized rhythmic patterns that help coordinate the ensemble tempo and additional aspects of the performance.

Kenong japan kettle gong and stand
Central Java, Indonesia
1840
Teak, bronze
Case: h. 43 cm (16 15/16 in.), w. 48 cm (18 7/8 in.),
d. 48 cm (18 7/8 in.)
Gift of Mr. and Mrs. Bradford M. Endicott and Mr.
and Mrs. Richard M. Fraser in honor of Jan and
Suzanne Fontein, and the Frank B. Bemis Fund
1990.552a–b

100

A variety of terms have been coined in the West to describe the music of the *gamelan*. The expression "heterophony" is perhaps the most descriptive. The term —which is also applied to many other types of Asian music—indicates the use of a single melodic line (without any harmonic implications) that forms the underlying musical material for the ensemble. In Javanese, this basic melody is called *balungan*, or skeleton. Yet a great musical richness is achieved by the way in which the melodic line is applied to each instrumental part. Each player performs the melodic line and ornaments it, adds passing tones, and uses octave duplications in a manner idiomatic to the instrument. This results in surface variety while the overall sharing of the melody achieves a powerful musical unity, underscoring the unified communal effort that goes into a *gamelan* performance.

101

***Rebab* fiddle**
Central Java, Indonesia (Surakarta)
Mid-19th century
Teak, ivory, buffalo bladder
L. 110 cm (43 1/2 in.), w. 43 cm (16 15/16 in.),
d. 11 cm (4 5/16 in.)
Frank B. Bemis Fund   1990.498a

South, Central, and West Asia

The regions of South, Central, and West Asia are interconnected by a number of musical traditions. With the exception of Tibet, they are also regions in which Islam plays a prominent cultural role, from North India to the Near East. Though politically part of China, Tibet is linked to these regions by its proximity to both South and Central Asia and by the preservation of archaic features of Central Asian music in Tibetan music. Tibet is isolated, however, from many of the musical trends that connect the rest of South, Central, and West Asia.

One of the primary features of the approach to music across this physical expanse, from North India to Turkey, is the tendency toward combination and synthesis of styles. This was seen as early as a millennium ago in the story of the tenth-century singer Ibn Bajja, who was based in Mecca (present-day Saudi Arabia). It was said that through his travels, Ibn Bajja had acquired an astonishing fluency in a wide variety of vocal and instrumental repertoires: tunes of Byzantium, the eight-mode system of Syria, provincial songs from Persia, and the music of the Persian *barbaṭ* lute. A similar circumstance is found in an often-quoted passage from the *Arabian Nights* that tells of the one musician who would be ready to perform, as needed, on a lute of Damascus (present-day Syria), a harp of Persia, a pipe from Tartary (Turkic Central Asia), or a dulcimer from Egypt.

It is not always easy to unravel the routes of the many mutual influences that occur over this broad area; they can work in all directions. This is especially the case in the interplay among the Iranian, Turkish, and Arab art-music traditions of West Asia. For centuries the musicians of West Asia have proven themselves to be eminently adaptable, drawing on resources of neighboring cultures to help meet the demands for musical change within their own local regions. This is also expressed in the adaptation of musical instruments. For instance, there are Turkish and Arabian versions of the Iranian instruments discussed on the following pages; similarly, there are Iranian and Arabian versions of the Turkish instruments. And it is from West Asia that musical styles and their instruments have traveled further still, to Europe and North Africa, as well as into South and East Asia; the adoption of janissary instruments from Turkey by European orchestras is just one example.

West Asia is notable for being the birthplace of three of the principal world religions: Judaism, Christianity, and Islam. As a result, sacred song and liturgy form a large part of the concept of music in that region. Musical instruments may sometimes have an uneasy relationship to this body of sacred music, with its primary emphasis on the voice as the medium of communication.

This ambivalence can be especially true in Islam. In many Islamic countries—in West Asia and elsewhere—instrumental music, and indeed any concept of "music" at all, may be deemed inadmissible by practitioners of the orthodox sects of the faith. The chanting of the Koran, which could in some cases be considered as artistically musical, is in fact viewed as the "reading" of this sacred text and not as music. The same is true of the call to prayer, five times daily from the minaret, which can also be highly artistic but is likewise not regarded as music. Before the twentieth century, however, some of these Islamic devotional practices were accompanied by musicians playing instruments. In some locales, either a drummer or a wind-and-percussion band would play for the call to prayer, utilizing the loud sound of the instruments to help draw attention to the activity. Similar ensembles might accompany the songs of pilgrimage.

Despite the uneasy relationship between the Islamic faith and the practice of music, music goes on. It has traditionally been an important part of festivals, especially weddings, throughout the Islamic world and is generally acceptable in that context (fig. 29). Folk music traditions, particularly in West Asia, tend to have strong regional identities, less susceptible to the intermingling that characterizes the art music. The classical music traditions are ultimately highly valued, requiring as they do an artistic execution of great refinement and subtlety. Central to these traditions is the ability to improvise: from India to Turkey, and beyond into North Africa, improvisation is essential. Just as musicians have adapted musical styles and instruments from neighboring cultures, so must they be fluid and adaptable in the very process of making music.

Fig. 29. Musicians, including players of horns, cymbals, and a wide variety of drums, accompany a wedding feast.

India

The Indian subcontinent—bordered on the northeast and northwest by a series of mountain ranges, and on the southeast and southwest by the Indian Ocean—is one of the most densely populated regions on earth, and India itself, a place of great diversity, is home to several languages. Its cultural traditions date back millennia and contribute to the richness of the musical traditions. Indian society is complex and stratified, with a system of hereditary castes affecting all levels of society, allowing different cultural groups to retain identity while existing together. The caste system traditionally has been able to accommodate cultural influx, such as conquering races. Several musical traditions are also caste-specific and hereditarily transmitted, such as the use of the *pūngī* double-clarinet by the snake-charming caste in North India. Traditionally, instrumentalists are men.

Hinduism and Islam are India's dominant religions. Although Buddhism originated in India, later to spread to East and Southeast Asia, its dominance in its home country has declined. Hinduism, once an influence in Southeast Asia, is now specific to South Asia, while Islam was first introduced to much of the area—by West and Central Asian invaders—during the early second millennium A.D. Ritual and ceremonial music abound in India (although some ritual music is not actually considered music, but simply an aspect of ritual practice). Many regional styles exist: devotional songs are found in many of the Indian languages and are associated with different Hindu cults. Many of these songs are of considerable antiquity. As elsewhere, music is ordinarily not included in Muslim worship, the chanting of the Koran being considered "reading."

In general, the music of South Asia is more akin to that of West Asia than it is to the areas to its east. The prevalence of plucked-string instruments is one important connection. The Indian art-music tradition is highly developed, has a strong basis in an indigenous music theory, and is transmitted by a disciplined oral tradition. There is an emphasis on the art of the soloist, and ensembles are therefore usually quite small, with only a handful of players. This means that, traditionally, performances are intimate, intended for a small number of listeners. Recent broadcasts over All-India Radio, despite bringing this music to an enormous radio audience, retain the sense of intimacy.

Fig. 30. A maiden plays the *bīn* zither in a *ragamala* painting representing the *ragini* called *Gujari*.

There are two "dialects" of Indian classical music. In North India, there is the Hindustani tradition, and in South India, the Karnatic. Hindustani music reflects many influences of the musical traditions of West Asia—such as Arabic and Persian music—while Karnatic music has been largely unaffected. This division between north and south was brought about by the introduction into India of Islam, which was primarily an influence in the north and brought with it many instruments from West Asia.

The art-music traditions of Hindustani and Karnatic classical music are, for the most part, improvised according to a traditional system of modal structures, called *raga*, and rhythmic structures, called *tala*. A *tala* is a cyclical temporal structure with a certain number of beats, a structure similar to—but generally more complicated than—the Western notion of meter. A *raga* is a form of a musical scale with a series of intervals that is unique to the given *raga*. The ascending and descending forms of the scale may vary, and certain groupings of notes may form the bases of melodies. A *raga* is defined not only by its selection of musical pitches but also by associations with a certain emotion ("emotion" is a basic meaning of the word *raga*) and with a time of day or seasons of the year.

In addition to being expressed musically, a *raga* may be expressed visually as a *ragamala* painting, in which an individual *raga* is represented by certain standardized pictorial elements. As the musical system of *raga* has both masculine (*raga*) and feminine (*ragini*) forms, *ragamala* painting may represent these by the presence of a prince or a lady. In a *ragamala* painting of the *ragini* called *Gujari*, for instance (fig. 31), a maiden is depicted holding a classical Hindustani *bīṇ* zither in her hands and waiting for her lover—both typical of the standardized iconography for this *ragini*. It is said that *Gujari ragini* should evoke an anxious mood, both musically and visually, and the sense of isolation conveyed by the maiden standing in a void certainly contributes to this.[13]

For many Western listeners, the music of India may be the most familiar

Fig. 31. A *bīṇ* player awaits her lover in a *ragamala* painting of *Gujari ragini*.

108

among the music of Asia. The influences of Indian music that found their way into Western popular music in the 1960s—perhaps most prominently in a handful of songs by the Beatles—contribute to this familiarity. More fundamentally, some of the principles that govern Indian classical music reflect qualities shared by Western music. These include melodic development, rhythmic tension and release, and underlying arch form (a general term for a musical texture that begins slowly and quietly, builds to a climax, and returns at the end—perhaps only briefly—to the characteristics of the beginning). These elements are, however, achieved by different means in Indian music. Melodic development is largely improvised, and cyclical rhythmic patterns effect tension and release; interestingly, both of these characteristics are present in jazz, though they are not typical in Western classical music. Arch form may be articulated over very long periods of time—what in a traditional performance of Indian classical music can amount to an entire evening.

This chapter focuses on string instruments of the Hindustani tradition, as these are most fully represented in the MFA collection and may be most often encountered by Western listeners. But the Indian tradition is also rich in wind instruments and drums. In fact, a remarkable aspect of Indian music is its emphasis on drumming; virtuoso technique is highly developed, with drummers traditionally enjoying a high status among musicians. The most familiar of the drums is the *tablā*, a pair of drums (consisting of one *tablā* proper and one *bāyā*) used in the accompaniment of most of the classical and light classical music of North India, in which a typical "solo" performance will include three instruments: the instrumental or vocal soloist, a *tambūrā* lute, and *tablā* drums. *Tablā* have become popular elsewhere in South and West Asia as the Hindustani tradition has become better known in these areas.

From a visual standpoint, Indian instruments can be some of the most sumptuously decorated in all of Asia. String instruments tend to take pride of place in their ornamental beauty, with extremely intricate inlay reminiscent of the patterns found in Indian architecture design. The *tambūrā* (p. 111) and *sitar* (p. 112) illustrated in this chapter, two principal lutes of Hindustani music, exemplify such decoration. Zoomorphic designs are also prized, with subjects ranging from the fantastic—dragon imagery is a favorite—to the real: the *mayūrī* fiddle is not only created in the form of a peacock, but is typically decorated with actual peacock feathers as well (p. 116).

Gintang

In contrast to India's many highly decorated string instruments, the *gintang* zither, a folk music instrument, is quite plain in appearance. The simplicity of this example and its lack of surface ornament are usual for the instrument. It is a different type of zither than the ones we have seen so far, but it may well be related to earlier zither forms in East and Southeast, as well as South, Asia. The type is known as a tube zither, as the instrument is constructed from a length of bamboo, hollow inside but sealed at each end by natural nodes of the bamboo plant. This example probably comes from Assam, in northeastern India, where there is a long-standing tradition of this sort of instrument. Similar tube zithers are also found further to the south, among tribal peoples in central India.

The *gintang*'s two strings are not made of a separate material attached to the body of the instrument but are actual segments of the surface of the bamboo, raised up from the tube and set to rest on small bridges that have been inserted underneath. Each of the strings is then further divided into two sounding parts by the attachment of a small, thin rectangle of wood, placed above the instrument's sound hole. The player, either holding the instrument horizontally in one hand or slinging it vertically over a shoulder, strikes the strings with a beater, creating a highly percussive effect without much definition to the musical pitches.

This simple kind of tube zither is viewed as a prototype from which other tube and stick zithers have evolved, growing in complexity by the addition of fur-

Gintang **zither and mallet**
India
19th century
Bamboo, wood
L. 55.3 cm (21 3/4 in.), diam. 6.3 cm (2 1/2 in.);
mallet: l. 21.8 cm (8 9/16 in.)
Leslie Lindsey Mason Collection 17.1782a – b

ther numbers of strings, frets, and resonators. Such a development is found at
a very early time in the Hindustani *bīṇ*,
the revered instrument of Indian antiquity (see fig. 30). The body of the *bīṇ* is a
long, hollow stick of wood—formerly
bamboo—reminiscent in a general way
of the body of the *gintang*. But on the
bīṇ, high wide frets have been added to
the basic stick form, allowing for the
bending of pitches. In addition, large
gourds that act as resonators have been
attached to the underside of the stick. In
contrast to the *gintang*'s two bamboo
strings, the *bīṇ* has seven metal strings:
four for melodic playing, and three for
drone pitches.

Tambūrā

Lutes, both plucked and bowed, dominate
the string instruments of India. The
tambūrā lute (fig. 32) provides the drone
accompaniment found in most classical
music, both Hindustani and Karnatic.
This large lute has a body made from a
gourd joined to a wooden neck and is
usually held upright by a player seated on
the floor. The metal strings (of which

Tambūrā lute
North India
19th century
Gourd, toonwood, ivory
L. 135 cm (53 1/8 in.), w. 40 cm (15 3/4 in.),
d. 31.5 cm (12 3/8 in.)
Mary L. Smith Fund   1992.259

111

Fig. 32. Three female musicians, the standing one
playing the *tambūrā* lute, accompany a *raja* playing
the *bīṇ*.

there can be four, five, or six—this example has four) are tuned to the fundamental intonation of the *raga*. The strings are never fretted, but are slowly strummed to produce an ambient drone as the accompaniment to a singer or a solo instrumentalist. Silk threads called *jīva*, or "life," are placed under the strings at the bridge to give the sound of the *tambūrā* a buzzing resonance that is considered aesthetically essential.

The name *tambūrā* is related to the names of several West- and Central-Asian lutes and, curiously enough, to the names of many types of drums (think of *tambourine*, for instance). Certain other, related lutes have a role that falls between the purely drone function of the classical Indian *tambūrā* and the purely rhythmic function of drums. The *tandūrā* used in the folk music of the state of Rajasthan, in northwestern India, is an example of such a lute: it provides drone pitches that are plucked rhythmically.

Sitar

Similar to the *tambūrā* in appearance and basic construction is the *sitar* lute, which is generally accompanied by the *tambūrā* in performance. The *sitar* is, however, a much more complex melodic instrument. Although its name means "three strings," the modern version of the *sitar* has five playing strings, two punctuating rhythmic strings (which the MFA example lacks), and about a dozen sympathetic strings. The presence of the sympathetic strings is the defining feature of the type of *sitar* used in classical music. The *sitar* player sits cross-legged on the floor, the gourd body of the instrument resting on the player's right thigh, while the neck—which is hollow and typically made of toonwood—extends upwards at a 45-degree angle. A gourd resonator is attached to the back of the neck on some instruments, but is not necessary.

The ancestor of the *sitar* was introduced into North India during the thirteenth century by conquering peoples from West Asia. Its name is derived from the Persian word *sihtār*, and the instrument is indeed related to the modern Persian *setār* (p. 136). Today, the *sitar* is regarded as the premier instrument of Hindustani classical art music, usurping the earlier central role of the *bīṇ*. Soloists garner great fame and popularity domestically and, in some cases, abroad: the musician Ravi Shankar is an excellent example. Many Westerners have been attracted to the sound of the *sitar*. The instrument even found its way into Western pop music, especially in a number of recordings by the Beatles of songs by George Harrison, one of Ravi Shankar's best-known students (fig. 33).

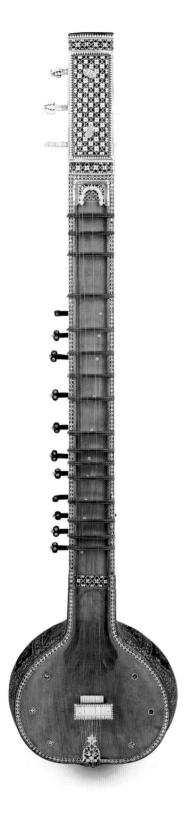

Fig. 33. George Harrison plays the *sitar* in Bombay, India, in January 1968. Seated next to him is British actress Rita Tushingham, who at the time was making a film in India.

Sitar lute

India (possibly Bikaner, Rajasthan)
Early 20th century
Gourd, toonwood, ivory
L. 118 cm (46 7/16 in.), w. 28 cm (11 in.),
d. 22 cm (8 11/16 in.)
Bequest of estate of Mrs. Dona Luisa
Coomaraswamy   1971.84

Sindhī sārangī

The most celebrated fiddle of Hindustani tradition is the *sārangī*, an instrument of compact appearance that is usually carved from a single block of wood. It is found in both classical and folk music in the state of Rajasthan, in northwestern India. There are several varieties of *sārangī* in Rajasthan; the *sindhī sārangī* fiddle is the principal folk *sārangī* of the Langa people resident in that state. Whereas there are three bowed playing strings made of gut (usually of a goat) on the classical instrument, the *sindhī sārangī* has two of gut and two of wire. Sympathetic wire strings are also used in great quantity on all *sārangī*, contributing to an ethereal shimmer in the instrument's tone; usually, thirty-six are included on the classical instrument and up to twenty-four on the *sindhī sārangī*.

The classical *sārangī* is played as a solo melodic instrument in the classical ensemble, where it is accompanied by a drone instrument—typically a *tambūrā*—and a drummer. Both the classical type and the *sindhī sārangī* may also be used in ensembles accompanying vocalists. The player of the *sindhī sārangī*—an instrument higher in pitch than the classical *sārangī*—accompanies himself, singing at the top of his vocal range. He is usually joined by a second musician playing the *gujrātaṇ sārangī*, which has more of a drone function.

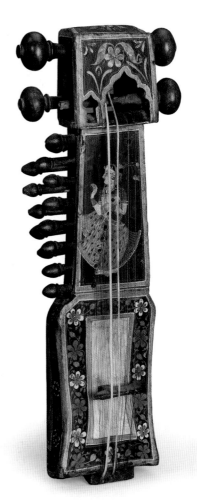

Sindhī sārangī fiddle
India (possibly Kotah, Rajasthan)
19th century
Wood, goatskin
L. 54.8 cm (21 9/16 in.), w. 14.8 cm (5 13/16 in.),
d. 9.8 cm (3 13/16 in.)
Samuel Putnam Avery Fund   1985.725

114

Practically all of the surfaces of the MFA's *sindhī sāraṅgī* are covered with decorative and figural painting. The two figures on the back of the instrument's body are especially suggestive of *ragamala* painting. Such figural paintings are not uncommon on string instruments of Rajasthan; similar decoration is found on a companion-piece five-string Rajasthani *tambūrā*, also in the MFA.[14]

Mayūrī

The *mayūrī* fiddle, another bowed-string instrument of the Hindustani tradition, is a more recent development than the *sāraṅgī*. Essentially a form of the *dilrubā*— a long-neck fiddle used to accompany

singing—the peacock-shaped *mayūrī* enjoyed some popularity during the nineteenth century but is now obsolete. The instrument can be designed with feet, as it is here, which allow it to rest horizontally in a position suggestive of an actual peacock with its tail feathers folded. When played, however, the *mayūrī* is held upright, as is the case with most Indian classical fiddles. In addition to being painted with peacock features and decorated with real peacock feathers, the MFA example includes figure paintings that suggest it originated in Rajasthan, in North India.

Although *mayūrī* players are occasionally depicted in old photographs, it is questionable whether the instrument ever

had much higher musical status than that of an attractive novelty. Nonetheless, the instrument represents India's national bird, which is found throughout the vast country and—as a symbol of beauty, grace, and fertility—often appears in Indian mythology, folktales, and classical song texts.

Mayūrī fiddle
India (possibly Rajasthan)
About 1800
Wood, goatskin
L. 95.6 cm (37 5/8 in.), w. 17.8 cm (7 in.),
d. 10.2 cm (4 in.)
Arthur Mason Knapp Fund   1983.411

Pūngī

Although many of the string instruments of India are ornately decorated, wind instruments typically are less so. This *pūngī* double clarinet, for instance, is starkly simple, though the shape of its bulbous gourd mouthpiece is certainly striking. The instrument is particularly fascinating, as it is characteristically associated with snake charming (fig. 34).

The bottle gourd of the *pūngī* has often been incorrectly described as a reservoir, supplying air to the reeds in a manner like that of the bagpipe. Actually, it is through circular breathing—a technique by which the player of a wind instrument breathes in through the nose while exhaling through the mouth—that a continuous wailing sound is produced on the *pūngī*'s two pipes, typically made of cane. Usually, one of these pipes is melodic while the other is a drone.

Snake charming is a traditional entertainment, its performance the hereditary domain of a specific snake-charming caste in northern India. Although the snake—often a cobra—seems to respond to the musical melody, it is apparently the movements made by the player of the *pūngī* to which the snake actually reacts.

The decline of snake charming, due in part to stringent laws concerning treatment of wildlife (pet snakes are now banned in India) and a general lack of interest by younger generations, has led to a decline in the playing of the *pūngī* as well.

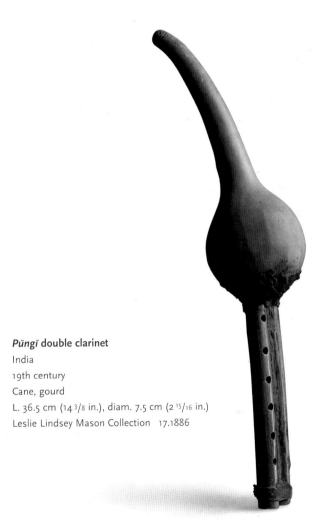

119

Pūngī double clarinet
India
19th century
Cane, gourd
L. 36.5 cm (14 3/8 in.), diam. 7.5 cm (2 15/16 in.)
Leslie Lindsey Mason Collection   17.1886

Fig. 34. A maiden plays the *pūngī* to the delight of snakes in a *ragamala* painting representing the *raga* called *Bhamarananda*.

Tibet

The Tibetan plateau, in the highlands of eastern Central Asia, is one of the most remote places on earth. It is home to a fascinating variety of instruments, made of rather unusual materials and in some cases of great size. Tibet's physical isolation has allowed the development of a unique music culture, and the instruments reflect this. The country's isolation also has meant that detailed knowledge of its music has only reached the outside world in recent decades.

From at least the first millennium B.C., the people of Tibet were nomadic herders, and during the first millennium A.D., the nation was an important political power in Central Asia. Tibet has had a long and complicated relationship with China, its neighbor to the northeast. In recent centuries Tibet had an ambiguous status as a suzerain state of China. After the establishment of the communist People's Republic of China in 1949, Tibet was invaded by the Chinese and brought wholly within the political domain of China. In 1959 the Dalai Lama, regarded by Tibetans as the spiritual and temporal ruler of Tibet, was forced into exile, and the government was

replaced with a dictatorship answering to the government of the People's Republic. With this, traditional Tibetan culture was suppressed, and some three thousand Buddhist monasteries were destroyed.

As a result of the political situation inside Tibet, many genres of traditional music are either no longer found there or are exploited to serve the political ends of the present Communist government. However, much of this music is being preserved by expatriate Tibetans. In many cases, it is exiled communities of Tibetans — in parts of India, Nepal, and Bhutan— who have introduced the country's music to the rest of the world.

Despite the present-day constraints, Tibetan music fulfills many of the functions that it does elsewhere: aiding religious worship, providing entertainment, and accompanying activities related to everyday life. The music of Tibetan Buddhism is the main religious music. Traditionally, Buddhist monasteries use a combination of vocal and instrumental music in both daily liturgy and special festivals of the ritual calendar. Several of the instruments are also used for calls to prayer and marking the hours. Many of these practices are maintained by expatriate Tibetans, and Tibetan Buddhist music has been highly visible to an international audi-

Fig. 35. The twenty-fourth Kulika king rings a *dril-bu* handbell.

ence through concert performances by touring musical groups and recordings.

The musical instruments that accompany this liturgical music include various kinds of trumpets (in a range of materials), oboes, cymbals, and drums. The wind instruments are always played in pairs, as are some of the percussion instruments. The melodic component of the ritual ensemble is contributed by the pair of *rgya-gling* oboes. The ensemble is loud and intense, and on first hearing, the music may seem somewhat chaotic. However, the awe-inspiring quality of this profoundly religious music cannot be denied, especially as it alternates with the quiet chanting of sacred Buddhist texts. As Peter Crossley-Holland, a scholar of Tibetan music, has written, "The monastery music, alternating between the loud orchestra with its complex texture and the soft, restrained, unison chanting, creates the sense of passing from time to the timeless, from melody to sounds-in-one, from sound to silence. It is the tonal expression for going beyond the world of names and forms to the Formless, which Buddhists hold to be the nature of the ultimate reality."[15] Indeed, the music, both vocal and instrumental, is considered by Tibetan Buddhists as a path to spiritual enlightenment.

Present-day Tibetan Buddhist practices reflect a blending of Buddhism imported from India with the earlier shamanistic practices of Bon, the indigenous religion of Tibet. Bon survives today primarily through an amalgamation of its forms with those of Buddhism. It is through Bon, which retains many features of practices that connect it with the shamanism of Central and even northern Asia, that the music of Tibet incorporates aspects of archaic Central Asian music. Animal symbolism is important in Bon, as it is in the hunting societies to the north. One story tells of how the drum used in Bon ceremony is transformed, through its being played by the priest, into a flying horse or deer, upon which the priest rides up into the heavens. The principal text of the unaccompanied Tibetan epic song tradition, "History of Gesar" (*Ge-sar sgrungs*), is related to the Bon tradition and involves similar animal symbolism: each of the melodies to which the epic is sung is referred to as a horse upon which the story rides. The Gesar epic can be found in various forms in Central Asia northward to Siberia.

Secular music, less familiar to many outsiders than the Buddhist ritual music, includes folk music, entertainment music for parties, and outdoor ensemble music. Tibetan folk music is primarily an unaccompanied vocal tradition, although the *gling-bu* double flute is very popular as a solo instrument. The party music is traditionally found at occasions both informal and official, and its performers may be amateur or professional. Songs for

122

dancing, drinking, and birthday wishes may be accompanied by a variety of secular instruments such as lutes, fiddles, and bamboo flutes. The outdoor drum-and-reed ensemble, utilizing *sor-na* oboes (which are related to the Turkish *zūrnā* discussed on page 147) and *lda-man* kettledrums, is very popular among resettled Tibetans in Ladakh, India. The music of these groups is used both for entertainment and for the accompaniment of festivities such as births and weddings.

Dung-chen

According to an origin story, the *dung-chen* long trumpet was invented by an eleventh-century king of the Kashmir area of western Tibet specifically to invite an Indian scholar to visit Tibet. The instrument, which is used in Buddhist liturgy, certainly makes an impression. It is the largest of the Tibetan instruments, comprised of three sections that telescope out to a fully extended length of about ten feet and can be collapsed for storage. The extended instrument is played with its bell resting on the ground. When the trumpet is carried in procession, the bell is supported on the shoulder of, or in a sling toted by, a second participant (fig. 36).

The *dung-chen* produces two deep, powerful notes an octave apart. Like all Tibetan wind instruments of the Buddhist ritual, *dung-chen* are played in pairs in the ensemble that alternates with chanting singers in the recitation of religious texts. They are also used for calls to prayer in the morning and evening.

Fig. 36. Tibetan *dung-chen* long trumpets are carried in a procession in Ladakh, India.

Dung-chen long trumpets
Tibet
Late 19th – early 20th century
Copper, silver
L. 303 cm (119 5/16 in.) each
Lent by Mr. and Mrs. Bradford M. Endicott

124

Thod-rnga

An unusual material used in the construction of some Tibetan ritual instruments is human bone—specifically the bones of people who have died violent deaths. Its use is religious and is intended to underscore the transitory nature of all life. The Tibetan *thod-rnga* skull drum is one such instrument, constructed from the tops of two human skulls joined at the crowns. Similar Himalayan double-headed drums are made from wood, in which case they are called *damaru*.[16]

The *thod-rnga* is a form of rattle drum. Held in the right hand, the instrument is rapidly shaken back and forth, causing the drumheads to be struck by two small beads attached to the tips of strings, themselves attached to the drum's frame. The instrument is used in Buddhist rituals, most commonly with the *dril-bu* handbell (fig. 35), which is shaken in the practitioner's left hand. The continuous and arrhythmic sounds of the rattle drum and handbell delineate sections of the ritual.

In Tibetan Buddhism, *thod-rnga* are associated with protective deities and are therefore regarded as tools for warding off evil. The cloth banner that dangles from the body of the *thod-rnga* is decorative and varies in color and design from one monastic sect to another.

Thod-rnga skull drum
Tibet
First half of 20th century
Bone, skin, metal, stone, silk
L. 80 cm (31 1/2 in.) overall; body:
h. 15.5 cm (6 1/8 in.), w. 12.5 cm (4 15/16 in.),
d. 13 cm (5 1/8 in.)
William Lindsey Fund, by exchange   2004.1

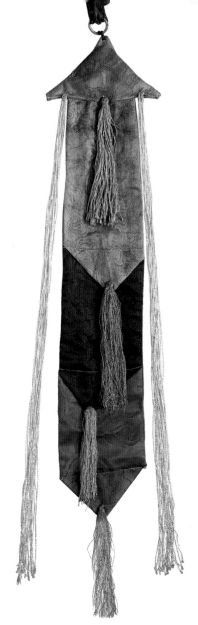

Dung-dkar

As popular trade items, seashells have long found their way inland. For millennia, the large marine snail called a chank has been revered on the Indian subcontinent and used to make shell trumpets. Hundreds of miles from any sea, chank shells are crafted into trumpets called *dung-dkar* for use in Tibetan ritual music.

To be converted into a shell trumpet, the chank may receive no more complicated a treatment than having the apex of the shell's spire removed.[17] However, the shell's surface is often ornately carved and decorated with silver and semiprecious stones. The MFA's example is unusual in that its surface is completely covered in silver, which itself receives elaborate decoration including both the eight Buddhist symbols (also known as the eight treasures, each symbolizing an aspect of Buddhist law) and the twelve animals of the Buddhist zodiac. As with the other wind instruments used in Tibetan Buddhist ritual-music ensembles, *dung-dkar* are played in pairs. The trumpet's sound—a single note—is loud and penetrating.

Dung-dkar shell trumpet
Probably Tibet
Second half of 19th century
Seashell, silver, semiprecious stones
L. 23 cm (9 1/16 in.), diam. 12 cm (4 3/4 in.)
Museum purchase with funds donated by
Michael D. Wolfe in memory of his wife
Elise Wolfe   2002.613

Gling-bu

The term *gling-bu* is used for various flutes in the Tibetan cultural area but is most commonly applied to the end-blown type, either single or double (as here). The end-blown flute is typically made of apricot wood, often with brass ferrules and bands that may, as in this example, receive some degree of decorative carving. Each flute usually has seven equally spaced finger holes; here the seventh pair of holes pierces the brass ferrule at the end.

Melodies for the *gling-bu* end-blown flute are pentatonic and unaccompanied. They tend to be very florid, especially on the double version. The *gling-bu* is popular among ethnic Tibetans and is one of the few instruments commonly associated with folk music, which is otherwise prima-rily vocal. Occasionally, the *gling-bu* is used by nomad herders to accompany songs.

Gling-bu end-blown flute
Tibet
19th century
Wood, brass
L. 39.5 cm (15 9/16 in.), diam. 2.2 cm (7/8 in.)
Leslie Lindsey Mason Collection   17.1825

Afghanistan

The Central Asian country Afghanistan forms a crossroads in the musical continuum between South and West Asia, and its music bears a complex relationship to both neighboring regions. Most of Afghanistan, a country the size of Texas, is mountainous, rugged, and isolated. It is an ethnically diverse nation: its majority population is Iranian (primarily Pashtuns); the next largest group is Turkic, and there are many smaller ethnic populations. Despite these ethnic differences, Islam is the religion shared by practically all Afghans.

The musical culture of the capital city of Kabul, in eastern Afghanistan, has looked to the Hindustani traditions of North India, making use of the *raga* and *tala* system and of some instruments related to those of India. The purely Afghan art-music traditions prevalent in Kabul, such as the singing of the highly poetic *ghazal* and the instrumental form *naghmeh-e kashal*, were influenced by Indian musicians active at the Kabul court in the mid-nineteenth century.

In western Afghanistan, by contrast, the music of the region surrounding the city of Herat in the Herat Valley has

Fig. 37. Two Afghan gentlemen are entertained by dancers and drummers.

drawn on the instruments and musical forms of nearby Iran. In the early part of the twentieth century Herati music intermingled with strong musical influences from Kabul. Today, prominent classical musicians are generally conversant in both styles and repertoires.

Traditionally, women are not involved in the performance of music apart from singing at domestic occasions, primarily weddings. With the exceptions of the *chang* jew's harp and percussion instruments used to accompany singing, women have not been allowed to play musical instruments. Although men largely have the exclusive and, in many cases, hereditary hold on the domain of music, especially instrumental music, this Islamic society has generally looked down on all music making, considering it to have a corrupting influence and to be essentially beneath respect. This has been especially true during the recent rule of the Taliban, when music and musical instruments were cruelly repressed, but it does reflect earlier attitudes as well.

Nevertheless, music has traditionally been considered indispensable for festive occasions such as weddings and holidays, and its use has generally been accepted for such contexts (fig. 37). Communities may encourage a certain amount of interest in music among their younger members, but generally only those adults who have become professional musicians perform in public. The combination of a societal persecution of music and the recognition of its importance in human activity has produced a complex situation for music in Afghanistan. The advent, in the middle of the twentieth century, of radio broadcasts of performances of Afghan music helped loosen the restrictive atmosphere, at least until the Taliban period.

130

Rubāb

Afghan music is dominated by lutes. One of the most important, the *rubāb*, is regarded as the national instrument of the country. It is a type of short-neck lute also found directly east of Afghanistan, in Pakistan and North India. The Afghan *rubāb* is understood to have emerged during the eighteenth century and has an important place in the major genres of Afghan art music—those of the capital city of Kabul and, more recently, of Herat.

The *rubāb* has a deep-set body and is therefore played horizontally on the seated player's lap. The instrument has three main playing strings of gut, together with two or three drone strings and more than a dozen sympathetic strings of metal. The gut playing strings contribute to an attractively dark and earthy tone color, contrasting vividly with the bright drone strings,

which are played rhythmically. The MFA's *rubāb* has the traditional four frets, also made of gut and tied onto the neck. As the *rubāb* came to be used in the music of Herat, two extra frets were added during the 1960s and '70s to accommodate variant intonations in Herati music.

In Herat the music of the *rubāb* consists of traditional song melodies. In the Kabul tradition the *rubāb* is often played with the rhythmic accompaniment of the *tablā-bāyā* drum pair, imported from northern India. In Kabul, the lute's repertoire typically comprises *naghmeh-e kashal* (a term translated as "extended instrumental piece")—improvisations upon *raga* and *tala* related to the musical style of North India and played in virtuoso solo performances. This association with the sophisticated music of North India has added still further to the popularity of the *rubāb* in Afghanistan. In North India the *rubāb* is used in folk music. The *sarod*, a similarly shaped lute with metal strings and a metal fingerboard—developed from the *rubāb* during the later nineteenth century by musicians from Afghanistan —has found an important place there in Hindustani art music.

"*Rubāb*" is a Persian word applied to a number of instruments found throughout Asia. The name (in various forms) is usually applied to fiddles, such as the splendid ivory Javanese *rebab* included in the *gamelan* Jati Mulyå (p. 101). It is also

Rubāb lute
Afghanistan
Mid-20th century
Mulberry wood, goatskin
L. 74.8 cm (29 7/16 in.), w. 14.4 cm (5 11/16 in.),
d. 17.5 cm (6 7/8 in.)
Gift of Joseph R. Coolidge in memory of his
wife, Peggy Stuart Coolidge   1981.773

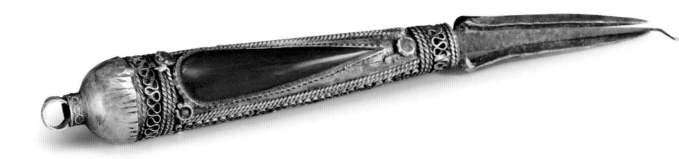

Chang jew's harp
Turkestan (probably northern Afghanistan)
First half of 20th century
Wood, copper, nickel silver, iron, colored glass
L. 19 cm (7 ½ in.), diam. 2.4 cm (¹⁵/₁₆ in.)
William Lindsey Fund, by exchange   2004.3

used for some lutes played without a bow, as in the Afghan _rubāb_. The indented sides of the body of the Afghan _rubāb_ reveal its ancestry as a bowed-string instrument, on which such indentations are necessary to allow for clearance of the bow.

Chang

The musical instrument commonly referred to in English as a jew's harp has a worldwide distribution. Despite this name, there is no conclusive evidence that connects the origin of the instrument

with the Jewish people. The jew's harp is a type of lamellaphone—that is, it is sounded by a long and narrow thin plate, or lamella, most often constructed from metal, wood, or bamboo. The player holds the instrument against his or her mouth, grasping the handle with one hand and plucking the bent tip of the lamella with the other. By varying the shape of his or her oral cavity, the player can achieve variations in musical pitch.

The jew's harp is especially widespread in Central Asia. The MFA example, called a _chang_, comes from Turkestan (traditionally the southern portion of Central Asia)—probably from Afghan Turkestan, the north-central provinces of the country. There, the *chang* is a common instrument and is produced locally by ironsmiths, who display the instruments with their other iron wares on sale to the public.

The handsomely decorated handle of this example is unusual. Typically, the handle is solely the continuation of the iron lamella, for a length about equal to the lamella. This handle, made of wood with inlay decoration of metal and colored glass, appears to have been a special addition, placed over the basic iron handle. The loop at the end seems to be for hanging the *chang*, when not in use, as an item of personal adornment.

The Afghan *chang* is played solo or in small informal ensembles with string instruments, where it provides a rhythmic rather than melodic accompaniment. It is generally associated with women and children players. In neighboring Uzbekistan, a similar jew's harp is played primarily by women in accompanying songs. In Uzbekistan the word *chang* is used for a hammered dulcimer—further exemplifying the variable use for many of the West- and Central-Asian instrument terms—and therefore in that country the jew's harp is called *changkobuz*.

Iran

Iran, alternately known by its traditional name of Persia, is one of the largest countries of West Asia and was the center of several important empires through much of its early history. After being conquered by the Muslims in the seventh century A.D., it was one part of a series of foreign empires. A number of ethnic groups populate Iran, many of which are separated from their kindred by the present political boundaries. For instance Baluchistan, the contiguous traditional domain of the Baluch people, is only partially contained within present-day Iran, the remainder being in Afghanistan and Pakistan. Islamic since the seventh century, Iran became an Islamic fundamentalist state following the deposition of the Shah in 1979.

Iran's art-music tradition has its origins in the imperial court music of ancient Persia. Little is known about this early musical culture, but the historical impression is that it was a highly developed art and that musicians were held in high regard. Following the Arab conquest of Persia and the introduction of Islam that began in the seventh century, Persian music and musicians were to have a profound influence on music throughout the Islamic world. The reciprocal Arab influence on Persia can be seen in the large number of Arabic musical terms brought into use in Persian music.

Shi'ite Islam became the state religion in 1502, at the beginning of Persia's Safavid dynasty, and in this orthodox atmosphere the attitude toward music—it was seen as frivolous—became hostile. The art-music tradition became more a private than a public activity, and ensemble music was discouraged. An emphasis on the art of the soloist remains, especially as Iranian art music is highly improvisatory.

String instruments, such as the *setār* lute and *kamānche* fiddle, receive pride of place in Iran and are used in the performance of music of great subtlety. Metal strings predominate in the art-music tradition, and the sonic effect is often one of shimmering waves of sound. The most important wind instrument in art music is the *nāy* end-blown flute, which boasts a profound antiquity in West Asia, particularly in Egypt. In the twentieth century an emphasis on drumming emerged, and drum soloists—performers of complicated rhythmic improvisations—have enjoyed a new prominence. Images of musicians in classical Iranian painting

Fig. 38. Two Persian musicians play a short-neck lute and a tambourine.

show a preference for small ensembles, often of a lone string instrument accompanied by a tambourine (fig. 38).

The compositions of Iranian art music—a repertoire known as *radif*, organized into twelve groups called *dastgāh*—follow a modal system called *maqām*. In a way similar to the Indian *raga*, a *maqām* is defined by a set of pitches that can have a particular melodic contour. In the art music of Iran, when existing compositions of the same mode are drawn upon for performance, they are arranged in sequences, or suites, according to the taste of the musician as well as the needs and context of the performance. Performers of such sequences of pieces may demonstrate their virtuosity in a number of ways, especially in their skill in modulating from one mode to another. The suite form also allows for drawing together musical materials from disparate sources, letting performers combine music from several cultural origins into an on-the-spot synthesis.

Many of the instruments of art music are found in folk music, a notable exception being the *setār*, presumably because of its light and delicate sound. Folk music accompanies festive occasions such as weddings and sporting events, often performed by the *sornā* oboe (related to the Turkish *zūrnā*) and the large *dohol* drum.

Setār

The long-neck *setār* is one of the two principal lutes of Iran; the other is the *tār*. Although its name means "three strings," the *setār* has had four metal strings since the nineteenth century. It is smaller and more lightly constructed than the other lutes of the *tanbūr* type (which include the Indian *tambūrā* and *sitar*) and is prized for its delicate tone color and rhythmic grace. These qualities are achieved by a strumming technique that utilizes only the right-hand index finger. The *tār*, in contrast, produces a more robust sound, its six metal strings plucked with a plectrum made of brass.

As with many of the Iranian instruments of art music, the *setār* is usually played solo or in the accompaniment of singing; only rarely is it found in ensembles. The detailed inlay of ivory (or bone), brass, and hardwood that decorates this example is typical of such art-music instruments in Iran.

136

Setār lute
Iran
Possibly 18th century
Wood
L. 78 cm (30 $^{11}/_{16}$ in.), w. 11.5 cm (4 $^{1}/_{2}$ in.),
d. 17.5 cm (6 $^{7}/_{8}$ in.)
Boston Symphony Orchestra,
John Barnett Collection

Kamānche

The *kamānche* fiddle is the only traditional bowed-string instrument of Iranian art music. Related spike fiddles range throughout Central and West Asia and up into the region of the Caucasus as far to the northwest as Georgia. The instrument has been established for several centuries in Iran. It is played there not only in solo performance but also in ensemble contexts, where its subtle tone color allows it to blend well with sounds of other instruments. In the accompaniment of a singer, the *kamānche* player follows the singer's melody closely, but not too closely; the effect is one of shadowing the singer, supporting the vocal line while not exactly imitating it, and thus adding depth to the overall musical end.

The *kamānche* is traditionally played with the performer seated on the floor (fig. 39) and—as with the Japanese *kokyū* and Javanese *rebab*—it is the instrument itself that is rotated side to side so that the strings come into contact with the bow, rather than moving the bow along the strings. The wooden body is distinctly spherical, carved from a single block of wood or made by joining several pieces. Sometimes the body is made from a

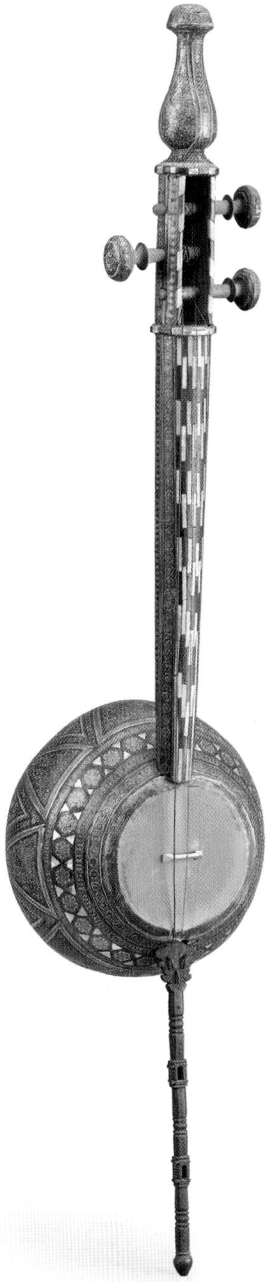

Kamānche fiddle
Iran
Possibly 18th century
Wood, sheepskin, ivory
L. 92.8 cm (36 9/16 in.), w. 17 cm (6 7/8 in.),
d. 17.5 cm (6 11/16 in.)
Boston Symphony Orchestra,
John Barnett Collection

139

Fig. 39. A player of the *kamānche* fiddle entertains a prince and a lady.

round gourd; this was probably the earliest method, later imitated by wooden construction. As with the *setār* and *dombak* goblet drum, this *kamānche* is decorated with intricate inlay.

Dombak goblet drum
Iran
Possibly 18th century
Wood, calfskin
H. 46.5 cm (18 5/16 in.), diam. 28.2 cm (11 1/8 in.)
Boston Symphony Orchestra,
John Barnett Collection

140

Dombak

The *dombak* is one of a variety of West-Asian goblet-shaped drums that were used in Mesopotamia as early as three thousand years ago. The goblet-drum type is generally known as *darabukka*, a term that appears to come from the Arabic word meaning "to strike." The *dombak* is the Iranian form used in art-music ensembles, where it has a long-standing role as the principal percussion instrument. In fact, many classical musicians also play the *dombak* in addition to their primary instrument. It is typically made from a single block of wood and given an intricate inlay decoration.

An additional large form of *dombak* in Iran is the *zarb*, which is made of ceramic and used to provide rhythmic encouragement during exercise in Iranian gymnasia.

Turkey

Turkey is the westernmost Asian country, whose occidental extreme is itself in southeast Europe. Modern Turkey is the successor to the vast Ottoman Empire, which existed from the late thirteenth to the early twentieth century. At its greatest expansion, the Ottoman Empire reached from Morocco to India and into southeastern Europe.

Turkish music has much in common with that of the rest of West Asia, sharing instruments, musical forms, and musical theory with the Iranian and Arabian art-music traditions. Turkish art music emerged from musical practices of the Sunni sects of Islam. In addition to its use in monasteries, art music was also found in palace performances (fig. 40). Compositions by known composers date back several centuries, the melodies composed in traditional modal forms called *makam* according to rhythmic patterns known as *usul*. These melodies, which do not come with any indication of the instruments that are to play them, are brought to life through the ornamentation added in performance by skilled musicians.

Turkey, as a predominantly Islamic culture, is subject to the general Islamic proscriptions against music. This attitude, dismissive of the use of music and musical instruments and indeed of the very aesthetic enjoyment of music, is traditionally more relaxed in the Sufi orders of Islam. In fact, music was traditionally an important part of one of the most familiar aspects of Sufi ritual: the ecstatic dance of the "whirling" dervishes of the Mevlevî order of Sufi Islam in Turkey. A form of meditation in movement, this activity captured the imagination of European observers as contact between the Ottomans and Europeans increased during past centuries. The Mevlevî dance rituals traditionally included—in addition to Koran recitations before and after the dance—singing accompanied by an instrumental ensemble of flutes, string instruments, and percussion. The practices of the whirling dervishes were widespread in Turkey until the twentieth century, when reforms restricted these Sufic activities and, in some cases, forbade them outright.

In addition to art music and religious music, folk music holds an important position in Turkish life. Turkish folk instruments are of great variety, with the *zūrnā* oboe occupying a favorite place. The principal string instrument is the *baglama*, a long-neck lute found in a variety of sizes. As Turkish folk music is

Fig. 40. A musical ensemble performs at a royal reception.

pronouncedly rhythmic, drums are of great importance; the *deblek* goblet drum and the *davul* bass drum are most highly regarded. Much instrumental folk music accompanies dance, and the pairing of the *zūrnā* oboe and *davul* bass drum is found throughout Turkey providing music for dance. Despite the huge number of different instruments, Turkish folk music is largely homogenous and tends to have only a limited relationship to the neighboring Arabic traditions.

In the eighteenth century, Turkish music was an influence on the music of Europe. The janissary bands—the military bands of the elite Turkish infantry—became known in the West through the late-seventeenth-century contacts between the Ottoman Empire and European powers. The bands consisted of wind and percussion instruments and, like many military-music ensembles, they played both on the battlefield to inspire soldiers in combat and at state ceremonies. The loud, aggressive janissary music was awe inspiring and proved during the later eighteenth century to have an effect on European classical music, especially that of Viennese composers.

144

'Ūd

The 'ūd short-neck lute is one of the premier art-music instruments of West Asia, existing in a diversity of forms and stringings from Iraq to northern Africa. Although 'ūd vary from country to country in West Asia and from maker to maker, the general type remains the same.[18] The Turkish variety is close to the typical Arabic form, though it is smaller by two to three inches in length and exhibits a slightly more rounded profile when viewed from the front. Traditionally, the 'ūd has been made with a variety of woods; it is sometimes said that the greater the variety of materials used in making the instrument, the finer its sound. The Turkish form has six courses: five string pairs, each pair tuned in unison, and a single string for the highest pitch. According to a label pasted on the interior of the instrument below the largest sound hole, this example was made in Constantinople, Turkey, by a Greek named Emmanuel Venios.

The West Asian 'ūd is understood to have derived from the Persian *barbaṭ*, a four-string lute current during the mid-first millennium A.D. From Persia the *barbaṭ* migrated both east to China (where it was to become the *pipa*) and west to Arabia (to become the *'ūd*). The Arabic word *'ūd* means "wood," and this originally meant the plectrum used to play the *barbaṭ*, later coming to mean the instrument itself. During the Middle Ages, the *'ūd* was introduced into Europe via Moorish Spain. The Arabic name with its definite article—*al 'ūd*—influenced the European name, "lute." The lute was the principal plucked-string instrument of western Europe until the later eighteenth century, by which time the European form of the instrument was strung with as many as thirteen courses of strings.

'Ūd lute
Emmanuel Venios (Greek, 1850–1915)
Turkey (Constantinople)
1899
Rosewood, black walnut, spruce, horn
L. 81.2 cm (31 15/16 in.), w. 36 cm (14 3/16 in.), d. 18.9 cm (7 7/16 in.)
Museum purchase with funds donated anonymously   2004.519

145

Kanun

The name of the Turkish *kanun* zither, one of the country's primary instruments of art music, derives from the Greek *kanon*, meaning "rule." This underscores the role of zithers in the classical world as instruments for measuring the size of intervals of musical pitch. The Arabic cognate is *qānūn*, and trapezoidal board zithers of the *qānūn* type are found throughout West Asia and North Africa. They seem to have made no impact in East Asia, where long zithers held sway.

The MFA *kanun* is strung with gut, in twenty-four courses of three strings each. The instrument is rested either on the player's lap or on a table, and played with two plectra, one attached to each index finger.

Although the history of the *qānūn/ kanun* stretches back some centuries (iconography goes back to the sixteenth century), little specific is known of it before the mid-nineteenth century, when it was subject to important developments in Turkey. One, the addition of the *mandal*, a series of levers underneath each string at the tuning pins, helped effect microtonal changes in the tuning of the strings to accommodate different Turkish modes. The lack of *mandal* shows the MFA model to be of the earlier type of *kanun*, which coexisted with the *mandal* type into the twentieth century.

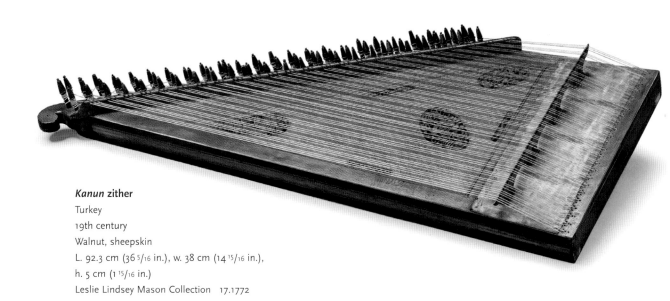

***Kanun* zither**
Turkey
19th century
Walnut, sheepskin
L. 92.3 cm (36 5/16 in.), w. 38 cm (14 15/16 in.),
h. 5 cm (1 15/16 in.)
Leslie Lindsey Mason Collection   17.1772

Zūrnā

Double-reed instruments like the Turkish *zūrnā* oboe range across the breadth of the Asian continent, from China (the *suona*), through Tibet (*sor-na*), to Iran (*sornā*) and Turkey, and indeed on into Europe (shawm). The *zūrnā* may be made from one of a great variety of woods; the use of apricot in these examples implies an eastern Turkish origin. Although these two examples are rather plain in appearance, it is often the practice to adorn *zūrnā* with additions of silver decoration.

The *zūrnā* is played with circular breathing—playing continuously while breathing through the nose. The young student of the instrument is trained in this somewhat counter-intuitive technique by means of a drinking straw: when a steady flow of bubbles is maintained in a glass of water, the student is on the right track. With the perfection of the technique, a *zūrnā* player using circular breathing is able to go on playing for hours, repeating and constantly varying melodies.

In Turkey the *zūrnā* is combined with the *davul* bass drum in festive music, often in lively meters of irregular numbers of musical beats, for outdoor public dancing. *Zūrnā* and *davul* are often used in wedding festivities (fig . 41)—"Without *davul* and *zūrnā* there can be no feast!" is one common saying attesting to the prominence of this music.[19]

Zūrnā oboes
Turkey
19th century
Apricot wood
Left: l. 29 cm (11 7/16 in.), diam. 5.7 cm (2 1/4 in.)
Right: l. 57.5 cm (22 5/8 in.), diam. 7.8 cm (3 in.)
Leslie Lindsey Mason Collection   17.1899
and 17.1900

147

Fig. 41. Players of the *zūrnā* oboe and other instruments participate in a wedding procession represented in a sixteenth-century Netherlandish woodcut.

Zūrnā of two different sizes (presumably equivalent to the two sizes shown here) were part of the janissary band of the Ottoman military—"treble and tenor," as noted in a document relating to the importation of a janissary band into Russia in 1725. Although double-reed instruments of the *zūrnā* type had entered Europe from West Asia during earlier centuries (the shawm is known from the thirteenth century onwards), many of the percussion instruments of the janissary band—cymbals, triangle, bass drum, and the visually ornate Turkish crescent[20]—were adopted by European orchestras of the late eighteenth and early nineteenth centuries. The vibrant style of the janissary music itself was adopted by art-music composers as well, as music "in the Turkish style" (*alla Turca*) became all the rage. Thus, a direct influence of this West Asian music may be found in such works as Mozart's celebrated *Rondo alla Turca* and Beethoven's *Marcia alla Turca* for orchestra, the latter incorporating some of the janissary-band percussion instruments along with European oboes and bassoons imitating the effect of Turkish *zūrnā*.

Notes

1. The many Asian languages are written in a large variety of scripts, and different systems of rendering native words into the Latin alphabet are available. In the interest of making the romanized Asian words included here as useful as possible for reference elsewhere, I have in most cases opted for the usage found in Stanley Sadie, ed., *The New Grove Dictionary of Musical Instruments* (New York: Grove's Dictionaries of Music, 1984).

2. The map accompanying the entry for "Dulcimer" in Sadie, ed., *The New Grove Dictionary of Musical Instruments*, 1:626, diagrams the instrument's extraordinary path.

3. Technically, Confucianism may more properly be regarded as a philosophy and Daoism's roots are also philosophical, but both are considered religions in a general sense.

4. This instrument is discussed in Stephen Addiss, with Kenneth J. DeWoskin and Mitchell Clark, *The Resonance of the Qin in East Asian Art* (New York: China Institute, 1999), cat. no. 7.

5. A. C. Moule, *A List of the Musical and Other Sound-Producing Instruments of the Chinese,* reprint (Buren, The Netherlands: Frits Knuf Publishers, 1989), 106; originally published 1908 in *Journal of the North China Branch of the Royal Asiatic Society*, v. 39.

6. William P. Malm, *Japanese Music and Musical Instruments* (Rutland, VT: Tuttle, 1959), 30.

7. Peter H. Lee, "From Oral to Written Literature," in Lee, ed., *A History of Korean Literature* (Cambridge, England: Cambridge University Press, 2003), 60–61.

8. The *rammanā mahōrī* is accession number 2004.404 in the MFA's collection.

9. A *sǭ ū* from the MFA's collection (accession number 1978.1204a–b) is illustrated in Darcy Kuronen, *Musical Instruments: MFA Highlights* (Boston: MFA Publications, 2004), 130.

10. The Mon are the same group as the Mon of western Thailand. In the Mon language the instrument is called *kyam*.

11. Robert Garfias, "The Development of the Modern Hsiang [*sic*] Ensemble," *Asian Music*, v. 16, no. 1 (1985): 3–4.

12. Margaret J. Kartomi, *Musical Instruments of Indonesia: An Introductory Handbook* (Melbourne: Indonesian Arts Society, 1985), 10.

13. Figure 30 is another representation of *Gujari ragini*, but other than one of the two female figures holding a *bīṇ*, it does not appear to follow the standardized imagery for this *ragini*. However, the darkness of this image may make reference to the association

of *Gujari ragini* with the rainy season. It should be noted that both of these *ragamala* paintings are from the Punjab Hills, far north in India and quite a distance from the more orthodox schools of *ragamala* painting.

14. The *tambūrā*'s accession number is 1985.725.

15. Peter Crossley-Holland, "Tibet," in Stanley Sadie, ed., *The New Grove Dictionary of Music and Musicians*, vol. 18, 799–811 (Washington: Grove's Dictionaries of Music, 1980), 18:804.

16. Another Tibetan instrument, the *rkang-gling* trumpet, is often made from a human femur, although some forms are made of brass. A late-nineteenth-century bone *rkang-gling* in the MFA's collection (accession number 1984.283) is shown in Kuronen, *Musical Instruments*, 78.

17. The nineteenth-century Sri Lankan *sak* in the MFA's collection (accession number 17.2170) is made from a chank shell in just this manner.

18. The spelling "*'ūd*" is the standard romanization of the Arabic term for this instrument, which is found throughout the Arab world. In the Turkish language—which uses the Latin alphabet—the word is spelled *ud* (or, occasionally, *ut*).

19. Quoted in Laurence Picken, *Folk Musical Instruments of Turkey* (London: Oxford University Press, 1975), 497.

20. See accession number 17.2043 in Kuronen, *Musical Instruments*, 31, for the last mentioned of these.

Glossary

bridge. On a string instrument, a construction that helps transmit the vibrations of a string (or strings) to the instrument's soundboard.

capo. A device that can be temporarily placed over the strings of an instrument of the lute type in order to shorten all of the instrument's strings at once, thereby changing the instrument's pitch.

course. On a string instrument, a grouping of two or more closely adjacent strings tuned to the same pitch (or to octaves) and plucked, struck, or bowed at the same time. A course acts in effect like a single string, but the doubling or trebling, etc., of the strings adds fullness and depth to the sound. When a string instrument has single strings in addition to such groupings, the single strings may also be referred to as courses.

dulcimer. A Western term for a form of board zither struck with light hammers. The term is often encountered, as this form of instrument has a wide distribution throughout the Eurasian landmass.

free reed. A type of reed in the form of a small flexible tongue, usually made of metal and fixed at one end. It is the sounding principle behind various East and Southeast Asian mouth organs.

fret. A strip of metal, wood, or other hard material placed on the fingerboard of a lute (or occasionally a zither) perpendicularly to the strings, in order to help define individual musical pitches.

gong-chime cultures. Southeast Asian musical cultures that feature ensembles in which sets of gongs, or gong-chimes, are a prominent part of the ensemble, often along with other metallophones.

heterophony. A term that describes a musical performance in which the instruments involved all play a single melodic line together, with each instrumentalist ornamenting the melody separately and playing in a fashion that is idiomatic to the specific capabilities of his or her instrument.

idiophone. A type of instrument in which sound is produced by creating vibrations in a sonorous substance from which the instrument itself is made. Idiophones may be struck, plucked, bowed, or scraped.

lithophone. A musical instrument made from stone. China has a long and rich tradition of the use of stone and jade in musical instruments. Lithophones are also prominent in Korean ritual music.

long-neck and short-neck lute. Describing a given lute as "long-neck" or "short-neck" is not always a strict matter of the actual length of the neck. The long-neck lute evolved from a type in which the body of the instrument, or a skin belly stretched over it, is pierced with a length of wood (originally a stick) that forms the neck. The short-neck lute evolved from a type in which the body and neck together were carved from a single piece of wood. There are instances of long-neck lutes with proportionately very short necks and short-neck lutes with necks of great length. Spike lutes belong to the category of long-neck lutes.

long zither. A type of zither specific to East Asia that typically has an extended, narrow body of wood or bamboo over which the strings pass.

lute. A string instrument in which the strings extend past the sounding body onto a neck.

metallophone. A melodic percussion instrument with metal keys. A word created to parallel *xylophone*.

mirliton. A thin membrane that is stretched over a hole in the body of an instrument and imparts a reedy buzz to the tone. It is the principle behind the sound production of the kazoo. For the bamboo wind instruments in this book, the mirliton itself is traditionally made of a piece of the thin inner part of the bamboo plant.

mode. A form of musical scale that has an identity and character distinct from other scales. Individual modes may be linked theoretically into an overarching modal system, which forms a resource of musical material for a composer or improvising musician.

pentatonic. "Five tones," as in a musical scale with five pitches, or pentatonic scale. Much of the music of Asia, as well as much Western folk music, utilizes pentatonic scales. Various configurations of musical pitches are possible in constructing pentatonic scales, resulting in many different musical possibilities.

plectrum. An object, usually small and often flat, used for plucking the strings of a string instrument, singly or collectively. Often called a pick, especially in the West.

short-neck lute. See *long-neck and short-neck lute.*

spike lute and spike fiddle. A type of lute in which the neck bearing the strings is attached to the body by passing through it, extending from the body at each end. Even though the neck may not be permanently attached to the body, this method allows the neck to be rigid in respect to the body. For a spike lute played with a bow, the term "spike fiddle" is often used.

sympathetic strings. Strings added to a string instrument that are not generally played directly, but which resonate "in sympathy" when the instrument's primary melody strings are plucked or bowed. Found especially on lutes and fiddles of South and West Asia.

xylophone. A melodic percussion instrument with wood or bamboo keys.

zither. A string instrument in which the strings extend the entire length of the sounding body.

153

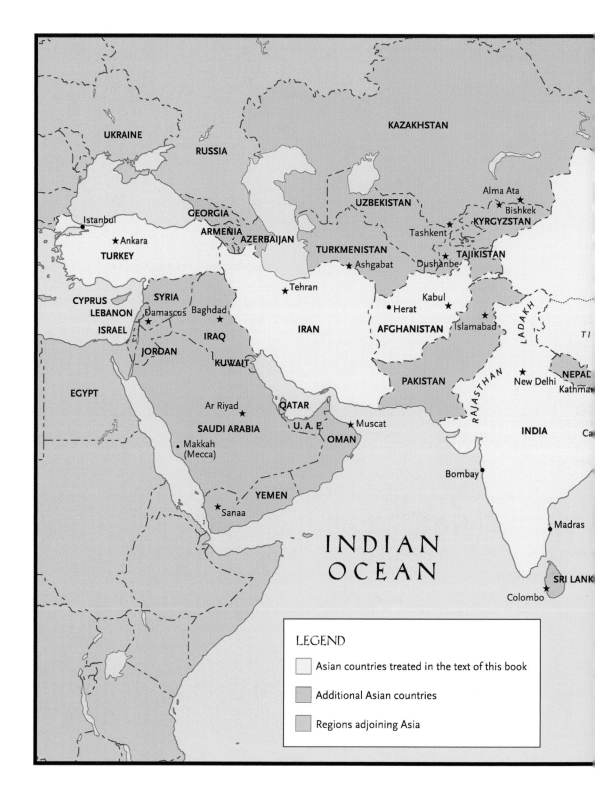

154

UKRAINE

RUSSIA

KAZAKHSTAN

Istanbul

GEORGIA

★ Ankara

TURKEY

ARMENIA

AZERBAIJAN

UZBEKISTAN

Alma Ata ★

Bishkek
★ KYRGYZSTAN

Tashkent ★

TURKMENISTAN

TAJIKISTAN

★ Ashgabat

Dushanbe

CYPRUS

SYRIA

LEBANON

Damascus

Baghdad

★ Tehran

Kabul
★

Herat

LADAKH

ISRAEL

JORDAN

IRAQ

KUWAIT

IRAN

AFGHANISTAN

Islamabad
★

TI

EGYPT

Ar Riyad
★

SAUDI ARABIA

Makkah
(Mecca)

QATAR

U. A. E.

OMAN

★ Muscat

PAKISTAN

RAJASTHAN

★
New Delhi

NEPAL

Kathma

INDIA

Ca

Bombay ●

YEMEN

★
Sanaa

Madras ●

INDIAN
OCEAN

SRI LANK

Colombo ●
★

LEGEND

Asian countries treated in the text of this book

Additional Asian countries

Regions adjoining Asia

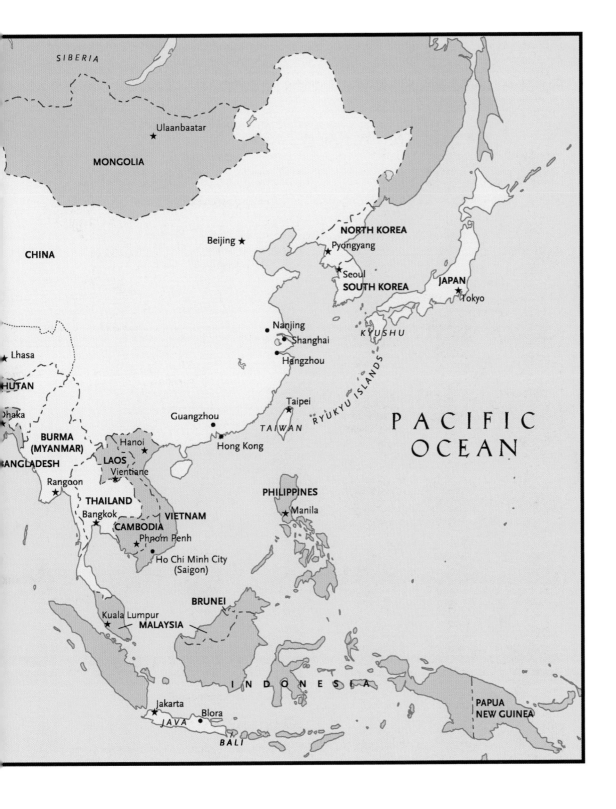

SIBERIA

Ulaanbaatar ★

MONGOLIA

CHINA

NORTH KOREA
Pyongyang ★

Beijing ★

Seoul ★
SOUTH KOREA

JAPAN ★
Tokyo

Nanjing •
• Shanghai
• Hangzhou

KYUSHU

Lhasa ★

HUTAN

Dhaka ★

BURMA
(MYANMAR)

ANGLADESH

Rangoon ★

Guangzhou •

Taipei ★

TAIWAN

RYUKYU ISLANDS

Hong Kong •

Hanoi ★

LAOS
Vientiane ★

THAILAND

Bangkok ★

CAMBODIA

VIETNAM

PACIFIC
OCEAN

PHILIPPINES

★ Manila

Phnom Penh ★
• Ho Chi Minh City
(Saigon)

BRUNEI

Kuala Lumpur
★
MALAYSIA

I N D O N E S I A

PAPUA
NEW GUINEA

Jakarta ★
JAVA

Blora •

BALI

155

Further Reading

General

Koizumi Fumio, Tokumaru Yoshihiko, and Yamaguchi Osamu, eds., *Asian Musics in an Asian Perspective*. Tokyo: Academia Music, 1977.

Kuronen, Darcy. *Musical Instruments: MFA Highlights*. Boston: MFA Publications, 2004.

Sadie, Stanley, ed., *The New Grove Dictionary of Musical Instruments*. 3 vols. New York: Grove's Dictionaries of Music, 1984.

East Asia

De Ferranti, Hugh. *Japanese Musical Instruments*. New York: Oxford University Press, 2000.

DeWoskin, Kenneth J. *A Song for One or Two: Music and the Concept of Art in Early China*. Ann Arbor: Center for Chinese Studies, University of Michigan, 1982.

Garfias, Robert. *Music of a Thousand Autumns: The Tōgaku Style of Japanese Court Music*. Berkeley: University of California Press, 1975.

Gemeentemuseum Den Haag. *The Ear Catches the Eye: Music in Japanese Prints*. Leiden: Hotei, 2000.

Gulik, Robert Hans van. *The Lore of the Chinese Lute: An Essay in the Ideology of the Ch'in*. 2nd ed. Rutland, VT: Tuttle, 1969.

Harich-Schneider, Eta. *A History of Japanese Music*. London: Oxford University Press, 1973.

Howard, Keith. *Korean Musical Instruments*. Hong Kong: Oxford University Press, 1995.

Liang Mingyue. *Music of the Billion: An Introduction to Chinese Musical Culture*. New York: Heinrichshofen Edition, 1985.

Malm, William P. *Japanese Music and Musical Instruments*. Rutland, VT: Tuttle, 1959.

Moule, A. C. *A List of the Musical and Other Sound-Producing Instruments of the Chinese*. Reprint with preface by Harrison Ryker. Buren, The Netherlands: Frits Knuf Publishers, 1989. Originally published 1908 in *Journal of the North China Branch of the Royal Asiatic Society*, v. 39.

Pratt, Keith L. *Korean Music: Its History and Performance*. London: Faber, 1987.

Provine, Robert C., Tokumaru Yoshiko, and J. Lawrence Witzleben, eds. *East Asia: China, Japan, and Korea*. Vol. 7 of *The Garland Encyclopedia of World Music*. New York: Garland Publishing, 2002.

Thrasher, Alan R. *Chinese Musical Instruments*. New York: Oxford University Press, 2000.

Wolff, Paul. *A Checklist of Traditional Japanese Musical Instruments*. The Hague: Haags Gemeentemuseum, 1988.

Southeast Asia

Kartomi, Margaret J. *Musical Instruments of Indonesia: An Introductory Handbook*. Melbourne: Indonesian Arts Society, 1985.

Miller, Terry E., and Sean Williams, eds. *Southeast Asia*. Vol. 4 of *The Garland Encyclopedia of World Music*. New York: Garland Publishing, 1998.

Morton, David. *The Traditional Music of Thailand*. Los Angeles: Institute of Ethnomusicology, University of California, Los Angeles, 1968.

Taylor, Eric. *Musical Instruments of South-East Asia*. Singapore: Oxford University Press, 1989.

Wolff, Paul. *A Checklist of Musical Instruments from the East- and South-east Asian Mainland*. The Hague: Haags Gemeentemuseum, 1989.

Yupho, Dhanit. *Thai Musical Instruments*. Trans. David Morton. 2nd ed. Bangkok: Department of Fine Arts, 1971.

South, Central, and West Asia

Arnold, Alison, ed. *South Asia: The Indian Subcontinent*. Vol. 5 of *The Garland Encyclopedia of World Music*. New York: Garland Publishing, 1998.

Cross, Thomas E. *Instruments of Burma, India, Nepal, Thailand, and Tibet*. Vermillion, SD: Shrine to Music Museum, 1982.

Danielson, Virginia, Scott Marcus, and Dwight Reynolds, eds. *The Middle East*. Vol. 6 of *The Garland Encyclopedia of World Music*. New York: Garland Publishing, 2002.

Jenkins, Jean, and Poul Rovsing Olsen. *Music and Musical Instruments in the World of Islam*. London: World of Islam Publishing Company, 1976.

Picken, Laurence. *Folk Musical Instruments of Turkey*. London: Oxford University Press, 1975.

Slobin, Mark. *Music in the Culture of Northern Afghanistan*. Tucson: University of Arizona Press, 1976.

Wade, Bonnie C. *Imagining Sound: An Ethnomusicological Study of Music, Art, and Culture in Mughal India*. Chicago: University of Chicago Press, 1998.

Suggested Listening

This guide is designed to help navigate the often bewildering number of recordings of Asian music, specifically identifying those that afford a good, representative sonic view of Asian musical instruments. It includes an overview of some of the better-known and most readily accessible record labels that release CD recordings of Asian music, in addition to a select discography of recordings that feature various Asian instruments.

Record labels:

Ocora (France) is the label of Radio France. Its world music catalogue is quite extensive and is consistently of high quality. In contrast to the UNESCO series, for instance, a given Ocora release will tend to focus on a performer or ensemble, usually providing several examples of a certain style and repertoire. Booklet notes are extensive and informative and are usually given in French and English.

The **UNESCO Collection** of world music recordings is truly international, extensive, and of high quality. The series is currently handled in France by Auvidis and is now also offered in the United States in Rounder's *Anthology of World Music* series. A UNESCO-Collection release tends to give examples of different repertoires without focusing on a single performer or ensemble. Booklet notes

are given in French and English by Auvidis, and in English only by Rounder, and are often briefer and more general than Ocora's. Additionally, Rounder has many other world music releases. Of particular interest are the various releases of historical recordings.

The United States–based **Nonesuch *Explorer* Series** is an important body of recordings of music made around the world over the last four decades. Much of the series has been rereleased on CD, and recently the Indonesian and South Pacific recordings have been rereleased in a uniform series. These mid-price *Explorer Series* recordings with extensive distribution are often the best place to start for world music.

Discography:

General

Instruments de Musique du Monde (Musical Instruments of the World)
Le Chant du Monde LDX 274 675 (France)
Thirty-six recorded examples (half of which are from Asia) covering all major instrument types; comes with a detailed and lavishly illustrated booklet

The Silk Road: A Musical Caravan
Smithsonian Folkways SFW CD 40438 (USA)

East Asia

China

Chine: Musique Classique (China: Classical Music)
Ocora C 559039 (France)
Classic 1950s–60s recordings of various solo instrumental music, including the *qin* zither, *pipa* lute, *erhu* fiddle, *zheng* zither, and many others

Li Xiangting (*qin*), *Chine: L'art du Qin (China: The Art of the Qin)*
Ocora C 560001 (France)

Lin Shicheng (*pipa*), *Chine: L'art du pipa (China: The Art of the Pipa)*
Ocora C 560046 (France)
One of the finest players of the *pipa* lute

Sizhu/Silk Bamboo: Chamber Music from South China
Pan Records PAN 2030CD (Holland)
Various chamber music genres

Tianjin Buddhist Music Ensemble, *Buddhist Music of Tianjin*
Numbus Records NI 5416 (UK)

Japan

A Collection of Unique Musical Instruments
King (*Music of Japanese People* series) KICH 2030 (Japan)
Includes recordings of several unusual and rarely heard Japanese instruments, such as the *kokyū* fiddle, *ichigenkin* monochord zither, *tonkori* zither of the Ainu people, as well as stone and ceramic flutes and whistles

Japan: Semiclassical and Folk Music
Auvidis (UNESCO) D 8016 (France)

Kinshi Tsuruta (*satsumabiwa*), *Japan: Kinshi Tsuruta*
Ocora C 559067 (France)

Ono Gagaku Kai, *Japan: Gagaku*
Ocora C 559018 (France)

Korea

Musique traditionnelle de Corée (Traditional Korean Music)
Buda (Musique du Monde series) 3016605 (France)

The Seoul Ensemble of Traditional Music, *Korea: The Seoul Ensemble of Traditional Music*
World Network 54.039 (Germany)

Traditional Korean Music, Sanjo and Vocal Music
King KICC 5191 (Japan)

Southeast Asia

Thailand

Royal Court Music of Thailand
Smithsonian Folkways SF CD 40413 (USA)

Thailand: The Music of Chieng Mai
Auvidis (UNESCO) D 8007 (France)

Burma

Green Tea Leaf Salad: Flavors of Burmese Music
Pan Records PAN 2083CD (Netherlands)

Inle Myint Maung (*saùng-gauk*) and Yi Yi Thant (voice), *Mahagitá: Harp and Vocal Music of Burma*
Smithsonian Folkways SFW CD 40492 (USA)

Java

Java: Javanese Court Gamelan
Nonesuch (*Explorer Series*) 9 72044-2 (USA)

Java: The Royal Palace of Yogyakarta; Instrumental Music
Ocora C 580068 (France)

Java (Sunda): Classical Music & Songs
Ocora C 580064 (France)

South, Central, and West Asia

India
Anthology of World Music—North Indian Classical Music
Rounder CD 5101-5104 (4-CD set) (USA)

Ram Narayan (*sāraṅgī*), *Inde du Nord: L'art du sarangi (North India: The Art of the Sāraṅgī)*
Ocora C 580067 (France)

North India: Instrumental Music; Rudra Veena, Vichitra Veena, Sarod, Shahnai
Auvidis (UNESCO series) D 8021 (France)
Various *raga* in order of associated times of day

Ravi Shankar (*sitar*), *Pandit Ravi Shankar*
Ocora C 581674 (France)

E. S. Shastry (*vīna*), *Inde du Sud: L'art de la vîna (South India: The Art of the Vina)*
Ocora C 580062 (France)

Tibet
Tibet: The Ritual Tradition of the Bonpos
Ocora C 580016 (France)

Tibetan Ritual
Auvidis (UNESCO series) D 8034 (France)

Recording of the *Invocation to the Goddess Yeshiki Mamo*, performed by the Lamas of the Nyingmapa Monastery of Dehra Dun

Afghanistan
Afghanistan: A Journey to an Unknown Musical World
World Network 56.986 (Germany)

Mohammad Rahim Khushnawaz (*rubāb*), *Afghanistan: Le rubāb de Hérat (Afghanistan: The Rubāb of Herat)*
VDE-Gallo CD-699 (Switzerland)

Rahim Khushnawaz (*rubāb*) and Gada Mohammad (*dutār*), *Afghanistan: Rubāb and Dutār*
Ocora C 560080 (France)

Iran
D. Chemirani, et al., *Musique Iranienne (Iranian Music)*
Harmonia Mundi HMA 190391 (France)
Solos on various classical instruments

Turkey
Münir Nurettin Beken, *The Art of the Turkish Ud*
Rounder CD 1135 (USA)

Nezih Uzel (voice and drum) and Kudsi Erguner (*ney*), *Turkey: Sufi Music; Ilâhi and Nefes*
Inedit CD W 260021 (France)

Figure Illustrations

Fig. 1. Detail from Muhammadi, *Hamza Mirza Entertained*, Iran, Safavid dynasty, second half of 16th century, opaque watercolor and gold on paper, Museum of Fine Arts, Boston, Francis Bartlett Donation and Picture Fund, 14.587

Fig. 2. Detail from an illustrated palm-leaf manuscript showing musicians accompanying a puppet play, Bali, 19th century, ink on palm leaf, courtesy of the Arthur M. Sackler Museum, Harvard University Art Museums, Gift of Philip Hofer, 1984.420, © 2004 President and Fellows of Harvard College, photograph by Katya Kallsen

Fig. 3. Detail from the *qin* composition *Qishan qiuyue*, from *Cangchunwu qinpu*, 1602

Fig. 4. Detail from Furuyama Morotsugu (active about 1688–1711), *Minamoto no Nakakuni Visits Lady Kogo*, Japan, Edo period, late 17th–early 18th century, hanging scroll: ink and color on silk, Museum of Fine Arts, Boston, William Sturgis Bigelow Collection, 11.7652

Fig. 5. The array of hanging gongs from the *gamelan* Kyai Jati Mulyå shown at the performance that christened Kyai Jati Mulyå at the Museum of Fine Arts, Boston, September 1990

Fig. 6. Caravan crossing the Silk Road, detail of the map of Asia from the *Catalan Atlas*, Spain (Majorca), 14th century, illuminated manuscript on parchment, Kunstbibliothek,

Staatliche Museen zu Berlin, Germany, © Bildarchiv Preussischer Kulturbesitz / Art Resource, NY

Fig. 7. Tomb figure of a camel carrying two forms of the *pipa* lute, China, Sui dynasty, early 7th century, earthenware with ivory-white glaze and applied motif, Museum of Fine Arts, Boston, Charles Bain Hoyt Collection, 50.897

Fig. 8. Jixiang Studio, *Yangqin* dulcimer, China (probably Guangzhou), 19th century, paulownia and other woods, Museum of Fine Arts, Boston, Leslie Lindsey Mason Collection, 17.2064

Fig. 9. Francis Galpin and his "Japanese Orchestra," vintage photograph from the album *Pictures of Players on Musical Instruments in Many Countries*, compiled by (or for) Mary Brown and donated to the MFA in 1918 by Mrs. Edward C. Moore

Fig. 10. Detail from Qiu Ying (about 1494–about 1552), *Harp Player in a Pavilion*, China, Ming dynasty, early 16th century, ink and color on silk, Museum of Fine Arts, Boston, Special Chinese and Japanese Fund, 12.887

Fig. 11. Detail from Fei Danxu (1801–1850), *Enjoying Music opposite a Waterfall*, China, Qing dynasty, 19th century, ink and light color on paper, Museum of Fine Arts, Boston, Gift of John Del Drago, 47.412

162

Fig. 12. Two details from a belt with seven jade plaques, China, Sui dynasty, 6th century, jade plaques and silver buckle, Museum of Fine Arts, Boston, Marshall H. Gould Fund, 58.692c and 58.692g

Fig. 13. Detail from *Fourteen Portraits of the Daoist Priest Wu Quanjie from 43 to 63 Years Old*, attributed to Chen Zhitian, China, second half of the 14th century, handscroll: ink and color on silk, Museum of Fine Arts, Boston, Gift of Mrs. Richard E. Danielson, 46.252

Fig. 14. Detail from Gu Jianlong (1606–after 1686), *Strolling Musicians*, China, Qing dynasty, mid-17th century, ink and color on silk, Museum of Fine Arts, Boston, Julia Bradford Huntington James Fund, 08.88

Fig. 15. Hedda Morrison (German, 1908–1991), A street entertainer blowing a *suona* to attract an audience for a performance of trained hamsters, Beijing, China, about 1933–46, photograph, Hedda Morrison Collection, Harvard-Yenching Library, Harvard University, © 2004 by the President and Fellows of Harvard College

Fig. 16. Katsushika Oi (active about 1818–after 1854), *Three Women Playing Musical Instruments*, Japan, Edo period, second quarter of 19th century, hanging scroll: ink and color on silk, Museum of Fine Arts, Boston, William Sturgis Bigelow Collection, 11.7689

Fig. 17. Detail from Suzuki Harunobu (1724–1770), *The Koto Player*, Japan, Edo period, mid-18th century, woodblock print:

ink and color on paper, Museum of Fine Arts, Boston, William S. and John T. Spaulding Collection, 21.4439

Fig. 18. Detail from Tosa Mitsuoki (1617–1691), *Benzaiten, the Goddess of Music and Good Fortune*, Japan, Edo period, 17th century, hanging scroll: ink and color on silk, Museum of Fine Arts, Boston, Fenollosa-Weld Collection, 11.4565

Fig. 19. Detail from a costume (*choken*) for the *nō* theater, Japan, Edo period, silk and gilt paper, Museum of Fine Arts, Boston, William Sturgis Bigelow Collection, 11.3926

Fig. 20. Detail from Suzuki Harunobu (1724–1770), *A Kamuro Uses a Mirror to Penetrate a Komusō's Disguise*, Japan, 1766, woodblock print: ink and color on paper, Museum of Fine Arts, Boston, John Ware Willard Fund, 45.833

Figs. 21 and 22. Details from *Immortals Arriving at the Banquet Given by Sŏ-wang-mo*, Korea, Chosŏn dynasty, late 18th–19th century, eight-panel folding screen: ink, gold, and bright colors on silk, courtesy of the Arthur M. Sackler Museum, Harvard University Art Museums, Ernest B. and Helen Pratt Dane Fund for the Acquisition of Oriental Art, 1996.142, © 2004 President and Fellows of Harvard College, photograph by Katya Kallsen

Fig. 23. Selected instruments from the *gamelan* Kyai Jati Mulyå, Central Java, Indonesia, 1840 and before 1867, Museum of Fine Arts, Boston, Gift of Mr. and Mrs. Bradford M. Endicott and Mr. and Mrs. Richard M. Fraser in honor of Jan and Suzanne Fontein, and the Frank B. Bemis Fund, 1990.498, 1990.538–598

Fig. 24. Detail from an illustrated Buddhist manuscript showing an ensemble of musicians, Thailand, 19th century, ink, color, and gold on paper, courtesy of the Arthur M. Sackler Museum, Harvard University Art Museums, Gift of Philip Hofer, 1984.523, © 2004 President and Fellows of Harvard College, photograph by Katya Kallsen

Fig. 25. Detail from an illustrated Buddhist text showing the Buddha-to-be fainting from hunger, Thailand, 19th century, ink, color, and gold on palm leaf, courtesy of the Arthur M. Sackler Museum, Harvard University Art Museums, Gift of Philip Hofer, 1984.502.4, © 2004 President and Fellows of Harvard College, photograph by Katya Kallsen

Fig. 26. A Burmese ensemble, vintage photograph from the album *Pictures of Players on Musical Instruments in Many Countries*, compiled by (or for) Mary Brown and donated to the MFA in 1918 by Mrs. Edward C. Moore

Fig. 27. The *gamelan* Kyai Jati Mulyå being played in its first performance at the Museum of Fine Arts, Boston, September 1990

Fig. 28. Selected instruments from the *gamelan* Kyai Jati Mulyå (1990.498, 1990.538–598, 1990.639–644), 1840 and before 1867, with some modern replacements, arranged on the Remis Auditorium stage at the Museum of Fine Arts, Boston, 1993

Fig. 29. *Marriage of Akbar's Brother at Agra in 1561*, India, about 1590, opaque watercolor on

paper, Victoria and Albert Museum, London, Great Britain, © Victoria & Albert Museum, London / Art Resource, NY

Fig. 30. Detail from *Gujari Ragini*, India (Jammu area, Punjab Hills), about 1700–1710, opaque watercolor, gold, and silver on paper, Museum of Fine Arts, Boston, Ross-Coomaraswarmy Collection, 17.3199

Fig. 31. Detail from *Gujari Ragini*, India (Punjab Hills), about 1700, opaque watercolor and gold on paper, Museum of Fine Arts, Boston, Ross-Coomaraswarmy Collection, 17.3200

Fig. 32. Detail from *Megh Malaraputra Saranga*, India (Rajasthan), about 1725, opaque watercolor and gold on paper, Museum of Fine Arts, Boston, Gift of John Goelet, 66.160

Fig. 33. George Harrison, lead guitarist for the Beatles, playing the *sitar* in Bombay, India, January 14, 1968, where he was visiting to record his music, © AP / Wide World Photos

Fig. 34. Detail from *Bhamarananda Raga*, India (Malwa), late 17th century, opaque watercolor and gold on paper, Museum of Fine Arts, Boston, Ross-Coomaraswamy Collection, 17.2913

Fig. 35. Detail from *The Twenty-fourth Kulika King of Shambala, Anantavijaya (Infinite Victory)*, Tibet, second half of the 17th century, opaque watercolor on cotton, Museum of Fine Arts, Boston, Denman Waldo Ross Collection, 06.330

Fig. 36. Tibetan *dung-chen* trumpets in procession, Ladakh, India, July 1992, photograph by Libby Ingalls, courtesy of Libby Ingalls

Fig. 37. Detail from *Reception at the Palace of Mirhab, Afghan King of Kabul*, probably North India, 16th century, opaque watercolor on paper, Musée Condé, Chantilly, France, © Bridgeman-Giraudon/Art Resource, NY

Fig. 38. Detail from *A Prince and Attendants*, Iran, Safavid dynasty, 16th century, opaque watercolor on paper, Museum of Fine Arts, Boston, Francis Bartlett Donation and Picture Fund, 14.584

Fig. 39. Detail from *Prince and Lady under Flowering Branch*, Iran, Timurid dynasty, 1425–50, ink, gold, and color on silk, mounted on paper, Museum of Fine Arts, Boston, Francis Bartlett Donation of 1912 and Picture Fund, 14.545

Fig. 40. Detail from *King Holding Reception*, Turkey, late 16th century, opaque watercolor and gold on paper, Museum of Fine Arts, Boston, Francis Bartlett Donation and Picture Fund, 14.621

Fig. 41. Detail from Pieter Coecke van Aelst (1502–1550), *Les Moeurs et fachom de faire des Turcs* (The Manners and Customs of the Turks), Netherlands, 1553 (based on drawings from the artist's trip to Constantinople in 1533), woodcut print, Museum of Fine Arts, Boston, Fund in memory of Horatio Greenough Curtis, M34928.8

Index